Building Critique
Architecture and its Discontents

Gabu Heindl
Michael Klein
Christina Linortner
(editors)

Ruth Sonderegger
Jane Rendell
Eyal Weizman
Nina Kolowratnik
Johannes Pointl
Pelin Tan
Matteo Trentini
Christian Kühn
Ana Jeinić
Liza Fior
Iva Čukić

ÖGFA
Österreichische Gesellschaft für Architektur
(co-editor)

Building Critique

SPECTOR BOOKS

Foreword

Any culture of critique is nurtured by the quality of its debates. These debates strongly differ from place to place. With this book, we want to add some new perspectives to a debate on critique within the field of architecture that has been predominantly led in the Anglo-American academic world. The scope of projects and contributors presented here spans a geographical area from the war-torn border between Turkey and Syria to London, one of the centers of financial capitalism. While each of the texts is situated in a specific place, they relate to the global power relations and transnational interdependencies that reach far beyond Europe. All of them link theory with practice in architecture and planning, their pedagogies and modes of production.

The idea for this book developed from the symposium "Kritik oder Krise. Haltung, Verantwortung, Widerspruch in Architektur und Stadtplanung" ("Critique or Crises. Attitude, responsibility and contradiction in architecture and urban planning"), which took place at the Sigmund Freud Museum in Vienna in October 2015. The symposium was a part of the year-long series of events celebrating the 50th anniversary of the Austrian Society for Architecture (ÖGFA—Österreichische Gesellschaft für Architektur). The ÖGFA is an independent architecture association in Vienna, founded as a critical voice aiming to distribute and debate architectural culture to and with a wider public beyond merely the professional audience. With this conference, we addressed questions concerning the current state of critique. The spectrum of the conference reflected many critical debates, material and immaterial formats, and networks of actors and their strategies around the central question: Has critique lost its power, or aren't there ever more reasons and fields of actions for a critical practice?

This publication would not have been possible without the support of a large group of people. First of all, we would like to thank the contributors to this book for their work and patience during the editorial process. We also would like to thank all the participants who took part in the three-part symposium: Ernst Beneder, Herbert Binder, Robert Burghardt, Iva Čukić, Liza Fior, Ole W. Fischer, Waltraud Indrist, Ana Jeinić, Nina Kolowratnik, Christian Kühn, Stefan Kurath, Wolfgang Otter, Johannes Pointl, Angelika Psenner, Johannes Puchleitner, Jane Rendell, Ingrid Sabatier, Marion Starzacher, Stephan Schwarz, Ruth Sonderegger, Pelin Tan, Christian Teckert, Robert Temel, Birgit Trenkwalder, Matteo Trentini, Gunther Wawrik. For support at the conference, thanks to Anna Neuhauser, Caroline Wullenweber, Ute Wadischatka, Karin Harrasser, Lina Streeruwitz, Angelika Fitz, Heidi Pretterhofer, Manfred Russo, and the board of the ÖGFA. For financial support, we want to thank the Arts and Culture Division of the Austrian Federal Chancellery and the ÖGFA. Thanks to our copy-editor Rafal Morusiewicz, to graphic designer Christian Hoffelner, and to the team of Spector Books, the people from the printing company Druckhaus Köthen, Kevin Dooley, Anna Laner, Ralo Mayer, Nina Pintzinger and Drehli Robnik.

The editors, January 2019

fig. 1 Symposium "Critique or Crisis–Attitude, Responsibility, Contradiction in Architecture and Urban Planning," organized by Austrian Society for Architecure (ÖGFA), Sigmund Freud Museum, October 2015

Gabu Heindl
Michael Klein
Christina Linortner

A Critique of Practice or a Practice of Critique

The End of Critique

That *critique* is in *crisis* has been a recurring trope from various positions and disciplines for quite a while now. For a long time, critique has sided with various progressive, ahead-looking programs in politics, the arts and other social spheres. Strongly assigned to the project of enlightenment as the "emergence from one's self-incurred immaturity,"[1] critique has been the practice at the heart of various progressive currents. Today, the same critique is said to have stumbled into a crisis and to have ground to a halt. Some of the agents in the art of critique have even gone as far as to proclaim the end of critique.

This argument comes less in the sense of crisis as a constant necessity for re-actualizing the position of critique, its methods and forms of articulation, and more as a declaration of death, or at least a severe disease. Critique has lost its power and aims at the wrong target, it has run out of steam, as Bruno Latour prominently declares.[2] For decades, the task of critique and deconstruction has been to demonstrate that so-called *facts* are produced and constructed, to uncover their ideologically biased nature, and to show that facts are often naturalized and objectivized. However, when contemporary politics takes over the gesture of critique and deconstruction in order to accuse the fact of global warming of lacking scientific certainty, or when it makes use of deconstruction for its own questionable political agenda,[3] we do have a problem of critique eating itself. A further step is taken by those, be it in social sciences or the humanities, who distance themselves from a self-declared critical practice, which claims to unveil the self-delusion that makes the foundation of all social existence and that renders everything as a mere belief to be uncovered only by the critic.[4]

Obviously, one cannot declare the death of critique without reviving it. The debate around the crisis of critique, however, has brought about a series of fundamental questions concerning the forms and methods of critique, as well as the positions from which it might be articulated.

The crisis of critique has come in different forms and shapes, having an impact also on the fields of architecture, art, and other forms of creative production. In recent years, there has been an ongoing change in the old forms of critique: a considerable number of journals within the established forms of disciplinary criticism that relied on journalism have been closed down. With design journalism being superseded by online reports, lifestyle coverage, smooth renderings, and promotional writing, also criticism faces a hard time. At the same time, there has never been a wider critical discourse in architecture in terms of publications, exhibitions, festivals, and events. Often, this sort of critique forgoes the criticism of disciplinary autonomy in exchange for a discussion of architecture, of the role of the arts in today's society, and of the role of both of them in drawing up alternative practices. Urban life has served as a key topic here, emphasizing the central role that cities and spatial production play in the formation of social life.

In respect to the crisis of critique, architecture differs from the arts, its neighboring field. Though this is not the place for an in-depth analysis of critique within the arts, it is important to summarize some of the arguments of the debate. Among the manifold contributions to the discussion on artistic critique, Luc Boltanski and Eve Chiapello's "New Spirit of Capitalism" has provoked perhaps the most prominent debate.[5] Paralleling *social critique*, which targets the issues of injustice and inequality, the book describes *artistic critique* as a struggle for autonomy, authenticity, and self-realization. Artistic critique is said to have spurred particularly after 1968. The book presents it as a trailblazer of contemporary capitalism with the artist as a role model for the logics of the entrepreneurial self that renders self-realization as absolute and overcomes the separation of work and life. Moreover, because the arts were in such high esteem, the contemporary mode of production took over the precarious living realities of artists and helped establish the creative worker as the new poor. Boltanski and Chiapello's theses have entailed an extensive debate. The argument involved abridging artistic critique and the possibly overrated role of the arts—after all, the arts cannot be blamed for all precarious working conditions, not even in the creative economy.

All this is different with architecture, which has always been considered at the frontline of capitalist production. The figure of the architect is hardly considered a critic in an either social or artistic sense. The architect's life-style does not immerse in the narratives of the free subject of the artist. The architect's image is rather that of the entrepreneur—an industrious caste adjusted to long working hours and office labor. With regard to architectural production, Boltanski and Chiapello's critique demands revision. Against this background, the contemporary simulation of endless career paths and self-invention might have little to do with the artistic critique that it has been ascribed to, but it could have been easily born out of the architectural office with lots of ideas yet few commissions. Actually, the restructuring of labor was elaborated in the design office, which served as a testing ground in corporate practice: unpaid internship, for example, developed from apprenticeship out of the design office into today's corporate world.

Nothing describes architecture's complicit role in the contemporary modes of production better than *less is more*, which Mies van der Rohe introduced into architecture during the early 20th century. Arguably the catchphrase of modern architecture, *less is more* laid out a program in which stripped-down design and the language of mere reduction were to bring forth architectural quality. The structure of such thinking of bareness equals an aesthetic phrasing of the economization of production, i.e. the optimal use of minimized means. Moreover, to make *more out of less* or — one step further — *something out of nothing* evokes another recent practice: it is the narrative of austerity policies imposed on whole populations as a neoliberal form of governance, as a late remedy against the "squandering" of welfare states.

Critique, Criticality and Post-Criticality: An Architectural Debate

That, in spite of all good intentions, architecture has little critical capacity was the conclusion of the 20th century's most rigorous architectural critic, Manfredo Tafuri and the Venice School, having evolved around the Italian journal *Contropiano*. Architecture has little to counter and resist against the capitalist social order since it is necessarily entangled in it and always sides with those in power. Tafuri strongly opposes what he calls *operative criticism*, in which theoretic reasoning is "elevated to a planning guide,"[6] and which he denounces as subservient to practice. Following Walter Benjamin's argument, not the *attitude toward* but the critic's own position *within* should be at the center of a critical project. For Tafuri, it is a call to arms to radically demolish all myths of architecture, a renewal of historical critique, whose engagement was to remain distant from the practice of architecture by all means. During the late 1960s and 1970s, Tafuri developed a distinctively new approach in architectural historiography through an investigation of architecture as a product of its wider, contextual forces. The engagement of architecture and utopia, involving architecture as an instrument of social change through planning and housing, was initiated with the study of *Red Vienna*. Matteo Trentini's contribution in this book discusses Tafuri's research on the housing program of Vienna's social-democratic interwar period, in which he identifies architecture's incapacity in re-building society, an argument Tafuri lays out in detail in "Architecture and Utopia."[7]

It might read as one of the very paradoxes within the relationship of architecture and critique that Tafuri's work served as the cornerstone of *critical architecture*. Fueled by postmodern literary theory, *critical architecture* developed during the 1970s and 1980s around a series of journals, conferences, and institutions, with strong advocates in both design and theory.[8] Building on concepts of resistance, negation, and autonomy, *criticality* was an endeavor to translate theory into design work: an internal critique whose proponents questioned the domain's uncontested truths by means of the architectural project. Their works stayed safely off commercial and state commissions, following instead the quest for rigorous architecture in a conceptual dry-run on paper, in exhibitions, and with small implementations. With this retreat, however, the project lacked an engagement for meaningful change and involved gradual de-politicization. Architecture is a part of the social realm and thus cannot be reduced to a mere outcome of its context. Rather, it keeps an internal autonomy that gives space for resistance, if we follow the argument of the proponents of *critical architecture*.

Over the years, the architects' theoretical works, propelled by the project of criticality, found their way out of the exhibition space into the realized, built reality. And quite soon after, techniques of critique, like that of *deconstruction*, which architecture appropriated in order to question its own truths (of proportions, structures, and representations of power) paradoxically contributed to establishing what we know today as starchitecture. Here, language served as a means of recognition value to create the author-architecture of best-selling brands. More than once, such projects were accompanied by city-redevelopment for the benefit of markets and not their social environment.

The early years of the new millennium brought the rejection of *critical architecture*, which might have been the result of frustration with the applicability of criticality, together with what it had contributed to practice, or maybe also a fatigue of theory. The position of *post-criticality* came with an apparent rejection of resistance, the embracement of commercial architecture and the confession that "there is in the deepest motivations of architecture something that cannot be critical."[9] Moreover, it pointed to a shortcoming of its predecessors: while *critical architecture* might have commented on social developments, its hands were tied for an active intervention — it was socially weak, which even its proponents admitted. *Post-criticality*, on the contrary, emphasized the *projective* power of architecture and its capacity to draw up alternatives. From today's perspective, however, some aspects in the post-criticality debate appear as an attempt of an inter-generational demarcation, as Christian Kühn argues in his contribution. By retracing the key arguments and scrutinizing which arguments could be applied in today's questions around architecture and planning, "The Crisis of Criticality: Becoming Critically Projective" shows that the debates on criticality and post-criticality hold much in common.

Gradual Openings

The continuity in the above-summarized relationship of architecture and critique has been characterized by a gradual opening toward other domains and other lines of influence. Its obstacles have been identified and overcome through an exchange with other forms of knowledge. Given the longstanding relationship with theory, architectural critique has gained a momentum in an intense exchange with social theory and Marxism. Shifting its attention from representation toward contextual social forces co-producing architecture has allowed for an interrelation with sociology and geography,[10] all of which have converged into a growing body of urban theory. Here, the works of Henri Lefebvre have served as an important reference, opening the field of critique to everyday life and social struggles. The influence has not been limited to academic disciplines, but it has extended from continental philosophy and poststructuralism, to psychoanalysis and feminist theory, to media studies, creative writing, film, and pop music.

One of the more recent influences has come from the field of postcolonial theory, whose main focus is to uncover dependencies and power relations between the so-called center and periphery in order to change the standpoint of a universal view from a western center and to "correct it from the edges."[11] While, for a long time, non-western architectures had remained excluded from the official canon of architecture, the influential writings on power relations that stressed the entanglement of built form and hegemonic structures challenged the way of looking at architecture in the colonial or post-colonial contexts.[12] Since then, a shift in scholarship has taken place, considering the transfer and migration of ideas, technologies, and styles not only from the Global North to the Global South, but also, increasingly, vice versa. Kathleen James-Chakraborty identifies four topics as particularly interesting for further surveys: "the comparative study of the architecture of empire, the recognition of the periphery as the location of innovation, the analysis of architecture as the locus of cultural memory, and the study of the way in which the fabric of European [...] cities is changing in response to the arrival of immigrants from the rest of the world."[13]

The current age of migration, as it has been called,[14] has led to new forms of cultural intermixture and to a pluralist, heterogeneous structure of urban societies. Consequently, most different cultural groups are forced to live side by side in today's industrialized metropolises. However, this does not mean that all human beings and cultural groups are considered equal in practice as they are in theory. Mary Louise Pratt terms these zones "contact zones"[15] — social areas in which unequal cultures collide within asymmetrical relations of dominance and subordination, spaces that always contain disparity, hierarchy, control, and resistance. In their contribution to this book, Nina Kolowratnik and Johannes Pointl discuss this asymmetry in the current European context. Drawing on the mappings and diagrams developed with students from TU Wien, they visualize the situation of arrival and the living conditions of asylum seekers in Austria against the background of the protocols and mechanisms inscribed into the system, reflecting upon what architectural knowledge can contribute to a critical debate of the current state.

The bigger picture of the processes shaping the contemporary world is of major importance for prospective forms of architectural thinking, involving aspects like migration and wars in various places. In her contribution, Pelin Tan reflects upon the challenges and possibilities of architectural pedagogy in the context of anti-colonial practices. Drawing on research done collaboratively with students working in and on conflict regions and engaging with their human and non-human environment, she stresses how architectural education could contribute to decolonial emancipative processes and to a criticism of the entangled power infrastructures of these environments.

One of the book's purposes is to emphasize that critique in architecture implies the need to take into account feminist perspectives. From the very beginning, since women were allowed to enter architecture schools, all of them have stood their ground, some with an activist feminist agenda, others coming by little or larger obstacles in their daily professional lives in a predominantly male professional environment, which more than often can feel hostile, if not sexist, and where women constantly need to prove themselves. Just as feminisms have evolved and changed, so have feminisms in architecture moved from the first and second waves onto what is now known as third-wave feminism, bringing forward intersectional and queer ways of thinking and prospects. As a recent surge of publications indicates,[16] such feminist practices are gaining new momentum, contributing to alternatives in architecture, design, and planning. And yet, even though women make around half of the graduates in architecture, both in schools and offices, the parity is still imbalanced, and the discipline still displays what can be called gender-illiteracy. This circumstance has spurred new and creative forms of criticism and initiatives, such as the parity talks at the ETH Zurich (a lecture series by predominantly female speakers, promoted by a number of posters featuring star-architects disguised as females[17]), the flash-mob protest of Voices of Women against the invisibility of female architects at the 2018 Venice Biennale,[18] and the Women Public Space Prague web-platform (WPS Prague).[19]

In order to address the manifold hierarchical structures in architecture, Jane Rendell suggests a "*critical spatial practice* to define modes of self-reflective practices which seek to question and to transform the social conditions of the sites in which they intervene, and test the limits of their own disciplinary procedures."[20] Such understanding of critique within architecture contributed to the conference *Critical Architecture*, held in London in 2004, and the book with the same title, which depicted *design* and *criticism* as part of an interdisciplinary field. While it showed the limits of the post-critical debate, the conference marked a cornerstone in the attempt of drawing alternative models of criticism and new critical practices. It opened space for more subjective positional approaches to rethink what design might effectively contribute and for practices that reflect their cultural context.[21]

Building Critique

What, more than a decade later, sets today's critique apart from the former academic ones, like that in the vein of criticality, is, probably above all, its engagement in the very sense of critical spatial practice. With architectural practice having found a way back to a more pragmatic, almost functional approach in addressing its issues, the same could also be said of critique. When raised in the context of architecture, today's social critique addresses its concerns in more direct and variegated forms. Often, this has developed out of an experience of political necessity: witnessing inequality, violence, and substantial changes within the urban environment, critics have stepped out of the safe haven of academia. Some of this critique takes on a role formerly attributed to activism rather than critique. Such a position might be taken both from within the academic context and from the outside; it is characterized not so much by a dimension of campaigning or organizing, but by following an open practice of exposure and speaking the truth.

A detailed reflection on truth telling as a practice of critique is part of Ruth Sonderegger's text about "professional critique." Against Kant's division between the obedient professional, on the one hand, and the critical citizen, on the other, she lays open other forms of vital criticism. Drawing on Michel Foucault's reconstruction of the Cynic *parrhesia*, of telling truth as an undertaking full of risk, of bodily practices of unlearning one's practices and, importantly, of failure, she shows that the art of telling the truth as a practice of critique always comes in many voices. The truth here shapes up differently from that of public intellectuals who appeared as holders of a fundamental truth[22] — it may be a weaker one, yet it shows itself in more nuanced shades. This is put into practice by Jane Rendell, who, in her contribution to this book, questions the independence of knowledge production in public universities in the face of third-party funding through mining companies. Written in a drama format, her text highlights the multiple voices and actors involved in the play of globally dispersed yet entangled realities, and it presents a reflexive form in which the truth develops between historical material and a person's speech.

The shift in relation to truth also manifests itself in the practice of Forensic Architecture, a team that, over the last years, has built on architectural knowledge for investigating state crime and violence. Truth is always produced, it is something that needs to be composed, as Eyal Weizman notes in the interview on the practice of Forensic Architecture. If, in the past, truth was considered to be a pre-existing fact to be found and uncovered, it is something fragile in today's approaches, something that needs to be carefully constructed. One might also say "built."

Critical spatial practice is a mode of action, a form of "critique as counter-hegemonic intervention." Political theorist Chantal Mouffe conceptualizes such counter-hegemonic interventions as a "critique as hegemonic engagement with" in opposition to "critique as withdrawal from."[23] On a fairly large scale, we currently observe a civic movement in Europe, which results in claiming democratic power in entire municipalities, such as Barcelona, Madrid, Valencia, and Palermo. Supporting each other under the label "New Municipality,"[24] these local governments stem directly from new social movements in their struggle against the neoliberal austerity politics. Their form of critique becomes urban politics, which also includes city planning that challenges the dominating urban governmentality.

It is the rise of urban citizen protests and movements that declares criticism against planning decisions not dead at all, much rather, critique in this emphatically active sense now finds itself displaced.[25] If not so much in media or universities, it can certainly be found in the streets or even in mainstream political debates. Many of the new rebel city movements have emerged from discontent with urban planning, voiced by a growing number of people. Such a case is presented in this book by Iva Čukić, who, as an architect, is part of the movement “Don’t Let Belgrade D(r)own,” which opposes an enormous profit-driven urban development along Belgrade’s central riverfront. Some of the most outspoken carriers of these protests are female architects, expanding their activism by getting involved in communal politics (from Belgrade to Barcelona). Current political constellations of conflict give a special urgency to an understanding of critique as active and practical, insofar as it is about developing alternatives to the existing status quo. Drawing from the definition of critique as a constant search for alternatives,[26] in her chapter Ana Jeinić reminds us that planning always aims at an alternative, and therefore it must be critical of existing conditions. Practice as critique is, in Jeinić’s sense, especially relevant in times of the current neoliberal “TINA” (There Is No Alternative) rhetoric, with the building industry and urban development playing a central role in free-market liberalism.

Creating alternatives is also inherent in the system of architecture competitions, in which many architects develop alternative proposals for specific sites and spatial programs. Yet, in such cases, the openness for such proposals depends on *open briefs* in a double sense: as openness to unknown results (hence not influenced) and as making clearly defined positions public, i.e. offering them up to debate and dispute. In fact, however, public-private partnerships and public task outsourcing result in project briefs formulated to maximize profit by investors and developers. Up until the turn of the century, it was a frequent practice in European architectural competitions to not follow the brief, which sometimes, if not often, led to success. If an architectural competition brief seemed wrong, some participating architects would change the parameters, thus changing the question they were asked to answer, so to speak. Today, such a creative practice of critiquing the conditions of architectural work seems untenable to the point that the entry would be dismissed. It becomes increasingly difficult for juries to embrace projects that do not fulfill the brief's requirements, due to the risk of lawsuits disrupting the planning process.

This is just one of the many starting points for architectural discontent, based on an acknowledgment of the general fact that "architecture depends."[27] Architecture is based on the contingencies of its context. It is entangled with hegemonic powers, often quite obviously so: after all, building activity is dependent on politics, on the accessibility to and ownership of the ground, on budgets, on building rights, and on much more. In its (co-)creation of the everyday built environment, architecture can also help to "build" and strengthen the very hegemonic power that it depends on. Criticizing architectural practice under current market conditions is not possible without looking at spatial implications of economic and social policy. And such implications can be overwhelming to the point at which planning practices and criticality appear to be two opposing things. Similarly discontenting is the way in which critique is all too easily incorporated into the very context which it meant to critique in the first place.[28] Tafuri's harsh diagnosis, discussed above, according to which architecture generally is functionalized by advanced capitalism, confronts us with a bleak picture: architecture seems to serve as a mechanism of the established social order, at best helping to soothe growing social inequalities. Now this could be understood as an injunction either to stop producing architectural work or to proceed with it while becoming uncritical to the point of cynicism.

Another all-too convenient way of dealing with the dilemma is to unquestioningly split the disciplinary role of architects doing their jobs from their political roles as citizens. It is a case of double consciousness: as citizens, architects might protest against the very political circumstances whose validity they support through their planning or building practices. Slightly differently, yet also operating in a split-consciousness practice mode, some large scale corporate offices "treat themselves" to an NGO part of their office which is cross-financed by their much larger body of uncritical work and functions as an excuse for that part of their practice.

However, a growing number of "critical practitioners," as they do not distinguish their critical position from their disciplinary operating modes, feel the need to confront dilemmas rather than to give up on them, and hence on critique. Acknowledging the dependency and contingency of architecture is paired with understanding one's critical architectural practice[29] to be a practice without fixed foundations. And yet, critical, also self-critical, architectural practice cannot and should not refrain from proposing partial and provisional foundations — which are produced through disputes and remain disputable.

Such modes of action can be manifold up to the moment that they imply decisive non-action. As regards the latter, architecture team Lacaton & Vassal is a good example with their 1996 project for the Place Léon Aucoc Plaza in Bordeaux. The result of their analysis was that the existing architectural context was just fine, so they decided, against the brief, that nothing, apart from minor maintenance work, was to be changed.

Another level of critical activity — being active in a non-compliant way — is a straightforward strike. This is a rare case in the architecture field, yet in 2015 in Vienna something close to an actual strike happened: a collective architectural protest on the occasion of the competition for a Viennese school as a public-private partnership-project (PPP-project). What caused the strike-like protest was the fact that Vienna's city government declared its intention to build ten large school campuses as PPP-projects, even though there were signals indicating that the government was aware of the disadvantages, especially for the public, of this financing model. However, in line with prevailing TINA rhetoric and split consciousness thinking, the city government stated that they had no alternative and that they were obliged to open the public task of building schools for the free market, citing the EU's Maastricht criteria. In the city government's view, this latter neoliberal agenda had to be followed no matter what, which implied that the government had to reduce public spending and instead stimulate private investments. During the school building competition under these conditions, some architects argued that their joining the competition would ensure quality standards as high as possible, thus making the most of a situation in which profit interests were dominant. Others publicly spoke out against joining the competition. A large group of architects and architectural offices (45, to be precise), however, participated in the manner of an activist strike. They all enrolled in the competition and, instead of handing in school designs, submitted contributions meeting the formal requirements, yet displayed various forms of creative graphic protest against PPP-projects. While the protest did not have much short-term impact, the continued critique of this and of other PPP-school-projects made Vienna's city government partly return to its older practice of open school competitions within public financing frameworks—which implied that education and its infrastructure were to be regarded as commons, not investment options.

While most of architectural production in Vienna is not commons-oriented but commercial, this city is still quite welfare-oriented and active in public building, and it still owns a large percentage of public housing. This is part of the "Vienna model" in urban planning and public housing that has gained world-wide recognition. And yet, even though the situation in Vienna is still a far cry from the effects that neoliberal planning politics have had on metropoles like London, the questions asked by the architectural office *muf*, based in the British capital, are valid in many places that might face a similar urban future: How is it possible for critical architects in disagreement with current conditions not to get excluded from decision-making processes — and not to exclude themselves? How does one keep "a foot in the door" in terms of both architecture and political hegemony? The practice which *muf* call "wedging the door" amounts to participation-oriented projects, however, not in a paternalistic way, but rather by making projects accessible to people who initially were not invited to participate. If democratic action involves critical practices of planning and building, then wedging doors, keeping points of access and borders, national or social ones, from being closed is an essential part of such Building Critique.

1 It is the phrasing in Immanuel Kant's *What is Enlightenment*, a source of critique, which has been taken up by Michael Foucault and Judith Butler.

2 Bruno Latour, "Why Has Critique Run out of Steam," *Critical Inquiry* 30 (2004): 225—248.

3 ibid, 226.

4 A position particularly distanced from the public critic in the figure of Pierre Bourdieu, as exemplified in: Luc Boltanski, *On Critique: A Sociology of Emancipation* (Cambridge and Malden, MA: Polity Press, 2011), and Jacques Rancière, *The Philosopher and His Poor* (Durham, London: Duke University Press, 2003).

5 Luc Boltanski, and Eve Chiapello, *The New Spirit of Capitalism* (London: Verso, 2017).

6 Manfredo Tafuri, *Theories and History of Architecture* (New York: Harper & Row, 1980), 149.

7 Manfredo Tafuri, *Architecture and Utopia: Design in Capitalist Development* (Cambridge: The MIT Press, 1976).

8 ANY, Assemblage, Oppositions, Institute for Architecture, and Urban Studies, to name some of them.

9 Rem Koolhaas, quoted in: Beth Kapusta, *The Canadian Architect Magazine 39* (1994): 10.

10 These two fields underwent a comparable disciplinary reinvention, working off its former instrumental governmental role.

11 Christof Hamann, ed., *Räume der Hybridität: postkoloniale Konzepte in Theorie und Literatur* (Hildesheim: Olms, 2002), 11.

12 Henri Lefebvre, Michel Foucault, Stuart Hall, Edward Said, and Gayatri Chakravorty Spivak, among others.

13 Kathleen James-Chakraborty, "Beyond Postcolonialism: New Directions for the History of Nonwestern Architecture," *Frontiers of Architectural Research* 3 (2014): 4.

14 Castles and Miller as quoted in: Leonie Sandercock, *Towards Cosmopolis: Planning for Multicultural Cities,* (Chichester: Wiley, 1998), 15.

15 Mary Louise Pratt, *Imperial Eyes; Travel Writing and Transculturation* (London: Routledge, 1992), 4.

16 See e.g.: Meike Schalk, *Feminist Futures of Spatial Practice: Materialisms, Activisms, Dialogues, Pedagogies, Projections*, (Baunach: AADR / Spurbuchverlag, 2017), Hélène Frichot, Catharina Gabrielsson, and Helen Runting, *Architecture and Feminisms: Ecologies, Economies,Technologies* (London: Routledge, 2018), journal issues: Meike Schalk and Karin Reisinger, eds., "Becoming a Feminist Architect," *Field Journal* 7, no. 1 (2017), and Meike Schalk and Karin Reisinger, eds., "Styles of Queer Feminist Practices and Objects," *Architecture and Culture* 5, no. 3 (2017).

17 → https://aaa.arch.ethz.ch/parity-html/.

18 → https://vowarchitects.com.

19 → http://www.wpsprague.com.

20 Schalk and Reisinger, "Becoming a Feminist Architect," 96.

21 Jane Rendell, Jonathan Hill, Murray Fraser, and Mark Dorrian, eds., *Critical Architecture* (London: Routledge, 2007).

22 As did, for instance, Jean Paul Sartre or Pierre Bourdieu, who showed a critique based on fundamental truth in public media.

23 Chantal Mouffe, "Critique as Counter-Hegemonic Intervention," online paper, EIPCP European Institute For Progressive Cultural Policies, → http://eipcp.net/transversal/0808/mouffe/en.

24 Christoph Brunner, Niki Kubaczek, Kelly Mulvaney, and Gerald Raunig, eds., *Die neuen Munizipalismen. Soziale Bewegung und die Regierung der Städte* (Vienna: transversal texts, 2017).

25 Thijs Lijster, Suzanna Milevska, Pascal Gielen, and Ruth Sonderegger introduce the notion of "displacement" with regard to art criticism in: Thijs Lijster, Suzana Milevska, Pascal Gielen, and Ruth Sonderegger, *Spaces for Criticism. Contemporary Art Discourses* (Antwerp: Valiz, 2015), 11—20 ("Introduction").

26 K. Michael Hays, "Critical Architecture: Between Culture and Form," *Perspecta 21* (1984): 14—29.
27 For reflections on architecture's contingencies, see: Jeremy Till, Architecture Depends (Cambridge Mass.: MIT Press, 2009).
28 Boltanski and Chiapello, *The New Spirit of Capitalism.*
29 For a useful (historic) overview of architectural practices with regard to critique, see: Tahl Kaminer, *The Efficacy of Architecture: Political Contestation and Agency* (New York: Routledge, 2017).

Ruth Sonderegger

Professional Critique?

My point of departure is a short text by Immanuel Kant that oftentimes has been considered as a founding document, if not the founding document, of the Western tradition of critique. The manifesto, whose exact title is "An Answer to the Question: 'What is Enlightenment?'" was first published in *Berliner Monatsschrift* in 1784 as part of a debate triggered by the question as to whether secular marriage was legitimate.[1] It was especially Michel Foucault's much quoted lecture "What is Critique?" (1978) that brought Kant's manifesto in favor of the Enlightenment back to life and made it attractive even for post-structuralist critical theorists who were more than hesitant to embrace Kant's "three critiques," which aim at a transcendental reconstruction of the a-historical preconditions of theoretical, practical, and aesthetic judgments. By contrast, Kant's "What is Enlightenment?" seems to advocate nothing but a historically specific and local, if not micrological, "attitude of critique," which Foucault, too, defends in "What is Critique?." In this lecture, he speaks of a "critical attitude," which he defines as "the art of not being governed or, better, the art of not being governed like that and at that cost."[2]

I will go back to Kant's short manifesto in order to, on the one hand, examine the relation between critique and profession. On the other hand, I will do so because I am convinced that even a brief discussion of the debate that Foucault unfolds between Kant and his own engagement with critique provides ample evidence that critique has not run out of steam as of late.[3] Much rather, such seemingly descriptive diagnoses, if confronted with Foucault's reading of Kant, reveal their declarative and, indeed, claiming nature: "Let's suffocate critique!."[4]

1. Foucault's struggle with Kant

The two central topics of Kant's manifesto are the reasoning "without the guidance of another"[5] and the preconditions of such reasoning: the freedom to articulate and to defend one's thoughts and claims in public. The Foucauldian "attitude of critique," however, plays a role as well in Kant's "What is enlightenment?," and it is indeed a double role. For together with the freedom that Kant advocates, he discusses the question as to which authorities may actually be criticized. Moreover, he engages with the challenge of whether and when human beings are self-critical, i.e. autonomous enough, in order to leave prejudice and guardians behind them. According to Kant, the autonomy of the critical subject of Enlightenment is all but a stable property. In Kant's view, there is only a process of enlighten*ment* but nothing enlighten*ed*. Moreover, the autonomy he advocates is not a question of knowledge but rather one of courage. It is not for nothing, as he contends right at the beginning: "The motto of enlightenment is therefore: *Sapere aude!* Have courage to use your own understanding."[6] Such courage, which turns out to be crucial also for Foucault's understanding of critique, needs to overcome two hurdles, according to Kant: "laziness" (Faulheit) in relation to oneself and "cowardice" (Feigheit) in relation to others. For, as Kant writes, "it is so convenient to be immature!"[7]

> "As far as emancipation from "immaturity" is concerned, Kant fully relies on the effects of the bour-

> geois public sphere and confesses: Thus it is difficult for each separate individual to work his way out of immaturity which has become almost second nature to him. [...] There is more chance of an entire public enlightening itself. This is indeed almost inevitable if only the public concerned is left in freedom. For there will always be a few who think for themselves, ... [who] will disseminate the spirit of rational respect for personal value and for the duty of all men to think for themselves."[8]

In order to secure such emancipatory public, Kant introduces a differentiation between the public and the private, which might appear as counter-intuitive to contemporary minds. According to Kant, the professional sphere of our job life is private and demands absolute obedience. The domain of public affairs, however, i.e. the sphere where the "man of learning" exchanges his views with other learned men, is the domain of critique. Here Kant writes, "by the public use of one's reason I mean that use which anyone may make of it *as a man of learning*, addressing the entire *reading public*. What I term the private use of reason is that which a person may make fit in a particular civil post or office with which he is entrusted." And, what is more, "[t]he *public* use of man's reason must always be free, and it alone can bring about enlightenment among men, *the private use* of reason may quite often be very narrowly restricted."[9]

On the basis of such a differentiation between an obedient private use of reason, on the one hand, and the public and critical one, on the other, Kant paves the way for a division that has been crucial ever since: one between what we are supposed and allowed to say in public as part of civil society and what we have to obediently accept as professional persons. Such a division is at play, for instance, when scholars, scientists, clerks, or architects insist on the division between their neutrality as job-related personae as opposed to their own (politically) involved points of view as citizens.[10]

It might appear as strange that Foucault questions neither this division nor Kant's account of the public sphere as the sphere of learned men.[11] It remains equally unsatisfactory that Foucault leaves unexplained the term "attitude," the central concept in his definition of critique in "What is Critique?". It is no earlier than in Foucault's last two lecture courses, taught from 1982 to his untimely death in 1984, that he revisits Kant's and his own account of critique as attitude.[12] The first of these two lecture courses, *The Government of Self and Others*, again takes Kant's answer to the question "What is Enlightenment?" as its point of departure. However, Foucault now blames Kant for betraying the principle of courage. Moreover, he accuses Kant of pessimistically over-emphasizing the difficulties of emancipation, which goes against the latter's opening claim that emancipation will almost necessarily evolve if human beings get the chance to exchange their views freely in public. And, what is more, Foucault criticizes Kant for entrusting one single individual, Frederick the Great, and his army with a process of enlightenment that is, moreover, conceptualized instrumentally as a means toward internal security. For Kant concludes his manifesto by assuring Frederick the Great that he "may say" to his subjects: "Argue as much as you like and about whatever you like, but obey!"[13]

Thus, there seem to be at least two beginnings of Foucault's engagement with critique, one in 1978 and another one in 1982, and in both Kant plays a central role. However, what connects both attempts is the concept of governmentality that Foucault started developing around

1978; this enabled him to make room for practices of critique and resistance, which, until then, had played only a minor role in his accounts of discipline and power.

2. The attitude of rejecting too much government

Foucault defines "governmentality" (from French *gouverner*, to rule or to govern) as the intersection of self-government, governing others, and being governed by others. In order to explain the term, he writes:

> "The contact point, where the individuals are driven by others is tied to the way they conduct themselves, is what we can call, I think, government. Governing people [...] is not a way to force people to do what the governor wants, it is always a versatile equilibrium, with complementarity and conflicts between techniques that assure coercion and processes through which the self is constructed or modified by himself. When I was studying asylums, prisons, and so on, I insisted, I think, too much on the techniques of domination."[14]

It was Foucault's engagement with forms of government in the aforementioned broad sense that enabled him to ever more clearly differentiate between power and violence. Versatile relations between being governed and governing oneself are relations of power. Stable relations, on the other hand, are relations of domination and violence. Whereas power relations presuppose subjects with agency, relations of violence passivate and culminate in extinction. In Foucault's wording:

> "A relationship of violence acts upon a body or upon things, it forces, it bends, it breaks on the wheel, it destroys, or it closes the door on all possibilities. [...] On the other hand, a power relation-

> ship can only be articulated on the basis of two elements [...]: that 'the other' (the one over whom power is exercised) be thoroughly recognized and maintained to the very end as a person who acts, and that, faced with a relationship of power, a whole field of responses, reactions, results, and possible inventions may open up."[15]

It is against the backdrop of such a differentiation between various degrees of mobility in relations of being governed, governing others, and self-government that Foucault introduces critique as an attitude, or, to be more precise, critique as the attitude of testing, criticizing, and transgressing oppressive tendencies toward stability in relations of power, relations that often go by the name of necessity and naturalness.[16] With his advocacy of mobility in power relations (as opposed to violent stalemates), Foucault provides a criterion to differentiate between constellations of more or less domination or freedom. However, the mobility that the attitude of critique defends may not be reduced to physical mobility. The neo-liberal imperatives of flexibility and innovation, for example, may become the climax of domination or immobility in Foucault's sense. Therefore, they can, and indeed need to be, tested, countered, and mobilized by practices such as stagnation, stasis, or "Reformpause."[17]

However, it is only in his last two lecture courses that revolve around *parrhesia* (truth telling, outspokenness, literally: all speech) that Foucault discusses the potential criticality of mobilizing power relations, or rather he stumbles upon a type of philosophical practice that enables him to concretize the attitude of critique: a practice that he deems worthy of taking up and continuing: *parrhesia*. Foucault's general definition of *parrhesia*, taken from his Berkeley lectures (1983), contends:

> "*[P]arrhesia* is a verbal activity in which a speaker expresses his personal relationship to truth, and risks his life because he recognizes truth-telling as a duty to improve or help other people (as well as himself). In *parrhesia* the speaker uses his freedom and chooses frankness instead of persuasion, truth instead of falsehood or silence, the risk of death instead of life and security, criticism instead of flattery [...]. That then, quite generally, is the positive meaning of the word *parrhesia* in most of the Greek texts where it occurs from the Fifth Century B.C. to the Fifth Century A.D."[18]

Against the backdrop of this and similar definitions of parrhesiastic truth telling, Foucault differentiates between three types of *parrhesia* in antiquity: (1) political *parrhesia* as part of the Athenian democracy's public debates, (2) ethical *parrhesia*, which consists in guiding and advising individuals, mostly friends, and (3) Cynic *parrhesia* — spelt with an upper-case "C," as opposed to cynicism with a lower case "c," which refers to various phenomena of modern relativism.

It is more than obvious that Foucault favors Cynic *parrhesia* over its political and ethical variants, for the ancient Cynics were a popular movement, probably the only non-elitist philosophical movement in antiquity that accepted women (like Hipparchia) and (former) slaves (like Diogenes). But there are at least three more reasons why Foucault is fascinated by Cynic *parrhesia*:

(1) Foucault admires the political militancy of Cynic *parrhesia*. On the one hand, "militancy" here means that Cynic truth-talk addressed not only a specific group of individuals — like political *parrhesia* that exclusively addressed Athenian men in possession of civil rights — or particular individuals in order to guide them in their efforts

to lead happy lives, as was the goal of ethical *parrhesia*. Instead, Cynic truth performances aimed at changing society as a whole. This implies a political universalism that was unheard of in antiquity. In addition, Cynic *parrhesia* was militant because it advocated aggressive, as opposed to reformist, ways of protesting.[19]

(2) The Cynics defended bodily truths with their bodies rather than with their minds. Such performative demonstrations did not play a role in any of the (more elitist) parrhesiastic practices. Ancient Cynics conceived of corporeal needs as normative in a twofold way. Bodily needs indicate what we are supposed to do: if a body desires sexual pleasure, it is ok to masturbate — even on a street, as Diogenes performatively argued. In addition, bodily needs hint at the rules as to what is not necessary and therefore should be rejected: a body does need shelter but not a palace or luxurious dresses, hence the legendary, but freely chosen, exercises of asceticism of the Cynics and Diogenes's constant references to bodily exercises in order to test whether such asceticism was still a practice of freedom or whether one was (already) governed by it.

(3) The Cynics developed a new, mainly anti-Platonic, practice of philosophy. Their basic assumption was that sophisticated knowledge and eternal foundations of shared values were not needed to change the world. A lot, if not enough, had been already said about equality, freedom, and truth. However, what was badly needed was the practice of a philosophical, militant life in light of these values. In advocating such life, the Cynics did not imply that the philosophical life was a simple application of established norms and values. They rather believed that the dormant provocations and excesses in concepts like freedom, equality, or autonomy would only come to the fore if we tried to live according to them, and thereby test and

possibly criticize or change the respective concepts together with their practices. A Cynical life devoted to such testing and trans-valuating customary norms needed to persistently unlearn habitual ways of thinking, doing, and feeling in order not to be governed by them, or to at least find out whether and to what extent one is governed. It is not for nothing that the Delphic oracle wanted Diogenes to "transvalue the currency," with currency — *nómisma* in Greek — meaning both customs and habits, on the one hand, and money, on the other. *Nota bene*, what cannot be changed through critical unlearning exercises is likely a relation of domination, not one of power.

As a consequence of their emphasis on practices of testing through unlearning, the Cynics did not bequeath many books to their possible successors. All we have is instructions wrapped in anecdotal stories and rumors about scandals and ridiculed heroes — the well known anecdotes about Diogenes's lantern, his public masturbation, etc. — which came down to us mainly via another Diogenes: Diogenes Laertius' *Lives and Opinions of Eminent Philosophers*.[20]

Foucault's reconstruction of the Cynical practices gradually turns into his own plea for such life. In following the Cynics and advocating their critical exercises, Foucault, on the one hand, acknowledges the oppressive power of everyday practices, much like Pierre Bourdieu, for instance. On the other hand, he contends that powerful customs can be changed and that mere reflection is not sufficient to achieve this aim. The existing habits need to be actively unlearned through both bodily and spiritual exercises. However, it should be noted that in contrast to the Stoic or Epicurean technologies of the self, which Foucault researched earlier as part of an aesthetics of existence, the bodily practices (mainly of unlearning) that he defends in his last two lecture courses, constitute a social-political, rather than individual, task.[21] For the starting point of the Cynical exercises are naturalized shared habits, whereby the difficulty to change them (individually) indicates the degree of social domination that lies dormant in them.

At first glance, there seems to be tension between, on the one hand, the Cynics' emphasis on aggressive temporary interventions that run the risk of certain macho-heroism[22] and, on the other, their commitment to continuous mental and bodily exercises. Or, to put it differently, an extreme modest attitude of accepting failure and trying again and again seems to be accompanied, or rather thwarted, by stories of exceptional actions of extraordinary courage and wit. However, together with the ancient Cynics, Foucault contends that it is precisely the sustained practical training for testing, criticizing, and changing bodily and mental habits that makes extreme interventions possible.

This is the point where Foucault's Cynicism intersects with Michel de Certeau's approach to everyday practices of resistance in his *L'art de faire* (1980), a study that takes much of its inspiration from the spatial practices of city dwellers that resist the strategies of housing programs and panoptical aspirations in urban planning.[23] This resistant potential of the seemingly most uncritical, indeed blindest, activities is what de Certeau holds against both the early Foucault of *Discipline and Punish* and Bourdieu's theory of practices. However, de Certeau might have conceived of resistant everyday practices as less ubiquitous, had he taken into account what Foucault discovered in the lives of the Cynics: that critique and resistance may, in principle, indeed occur everywhere, but that they neither are ubiquitous nor erupt out of the blue, being rather the result of relentless practices of unlearning.

In other words, Foucault's last lecture courses defend the engagement, both practical and critical, with everyday practices without discarding Bourdieu's insight that nobody contributes more fervently to oppressive habits than the oftentimes power-blind practitioners themselves. It is not for nothing that Foucault discusses the (ancient) practices of critical exercises in light of the imminent danger that such exercises — even exercises in undoing habitual practices — easily become, and indeed oftentimes are, tools of disciplining and thus the opposite of critique. In his eyes, exercises as such are, therefore, neither critical nor blind. Yet to differentiate between critical (i.e. mobilizing) and not so critical (i.e. hardening) exercises is all the more important as today's processes of subjectivation are based on various kinds of seemingly open-ended experiments of life-long learning. Therefore, it is imperative to find out how practices of unlearning can work against their innermost tendency toward habitualization. In light of this challenge, Foucault emphasizes both the Cynics' acceptance of failure and the open composition of their movement that spoke never with one voice but rather through many singular articulations. Both failing and being thwarted by other Cynics further the interruptions that are essential for practices of unlearning. In other words: the more spectacular performances of some Cynics cannot be severed from their less glamorous, and indeed tedious, daily exercises and failures.

3. Résumé

In Foucault's eyes, critique as an attitude articulates itself most convincingly in a Cynical life, a life of exercises that analyze where power has accumulated, on the one hand, and experiment with scandalizing and ridiculing accumulated power, as well as with unlearning one's involvement in them, on the other. Moreover, his lecture courses on *parrhesia* reveal that there is no part of society in which the attitude of critique might not be necessary. This is a clear critique of the Kantian division between the private and the public: between obedient professionals and critical citizens. Instead of making critique the business of philosophers, scientists, scholars, and other experts, Foucault highlights that all (more or less professional) fields of expertise produce their own naturalized power structures. Operating on the terrain of naturalized habits, critique as attitude therefore goes against the grain of the Kantian division of labor.

If we follow Foucault's invitation to think of critique as an attitude of unlearning everyday practices, the implications of contemporary diagnoses, according to which critique is in crisis, become pallid: implications, that is, according to which critique is authoritarian and elitist — criticism raised e.g. by Luc Boltanski and Jacques Rancière[24] — or miserabilistic and focused on negation and shortage, as Bruno Latour, Alain Badiou, Peter Sloterdijk, Thomas Edlinger, and many others have claimed.[25] Much rather, the Cynic critique, as presented by Foucault, is inventive and humorous. In addition, the accusation that such critique always turns into assimilation to the powers that be, and therefore is necessarily a trailblazer for ever more subtle forms of domination, comes to almost nothing. For as soon as a Cynical practice is assimilated into the dynamics of stabilizing power relations, the Cynic is elsewhere. She is not interested in eternity, not even in surviving as the one that she is at a specific moment.[26] Instead of securing what she has and is right now, she patiently desires more since, to cite Foucault once more, *parrhesia* is "the patient labour (that gives) form to our impatience for liberty."[27]

1 Immanuel Kant, "An Answer to the Question: 'What is Enlightenment?'" in *Immanuel Kant, Political Writings*, ed. H. S. Reiss (Cambridge: Cambridge Univ. Press, 1991), 54—60.
2 Michel Foucault, "What is Critique?" in *The Politics of Truth*, eds. Sylvère Lotringer and Lysa Hochroth (New York: Semiotext(e), 1997), 45. This essay was originally a lecture given at the French Society of Philosophy on May 27, 1978, and later published in *Bulletin de la Société française de la Philosophie 84*, no. 2 (1990), 35—63.
3 For such a diagnosis, cf. Bruno Latour, "Why Has Critique Run out of Steam? From Matters of Fact to Matters of Concern," *Critical Inquiry* 30 (2004): 225—248.
4 Sabine Hark has rightfully spoken of such a descriptive trick as "death by report." Sabine Hark, "Was ist und wozu Kritik? Über Möglichkeiten und Grenzen feministischer Kritik heute," *Feministische Studien* 27, no. 1 (2009): 22—35, accessed December 29, 2017. → http://www.zifg.tu-berlin.de/fileadmin/i44/DOKU/Publikationen/FS_Hark_Kritik.pdf. Cf. esp. the essay's first part entitled "Death by Report — Vorspiel."
5 Kant, "An Answer to the Question," 54.
6 Ibid.
7 Ibid.
8 Ibid., 54 f.
9 Ibid., 55.
10 Jane Rendell's case might indicate that currently scholars are no longer allowed to express their views as citizens in public if the object of the views expressed is the institution they are affiliated with (cf. her contribution to this book).
11 For an alternative, proletarian public, cf. Oskar Negt and Alexander Kluge, *Öffentlichkeit und Erfahrung. Zur Organisationsanalyse von bürgerlicher und proletarischer Öffentlichkeit* (Frankfurt am Main: Suhrkamp, 1972).
12 Michel Foucault, *The Government of Self and Others: Lectures at the Collège de France 1982—1983* (Basingstoke and New York: Palgrave Macmillan, 2010); Michel Foucault, *The Courage of Truth. The Government of Self and Others II: Lectures at the Collège de France 1983—1984* (Basingstoke and New York: Palgrave Macmillan, 2011).
13 Kant, "An Answer to the Question," 59.
14 Michel Foucault, "Subjectivity and Truth," in *About the Beginning of the Hermeneutics of the Self. Lectures at Dartmouth College*, 1980 (Chicago and London: The Univ. of Chicago Press, 2016), 19—51, 25 f, 198—227.
15 Michel Foucault, "The Subject and Power," *Critical Inquiry*, 8, no. 4 (1982): 789.
16 This is why, in his essay "What is Critique," Foucault gives the following much quoted definition of "the critical attitude": "[...] as both partner and adversary to the arts of governing, as an act of defiance [...], a way to displace them, with basic distrust, but also and by the same token, as a line of development of the arts of governing, there would have been something born in Europe at that time (= in the 15th and 16th century, RS), a kind of general cultural form, both a political and a moral attitude, a way of thinking, etc., and which I would very simply call the art of not being governed or, better, the art of not being governed like that and at that cost." Michel Foucault, "What is Critique?," 44 f.
17 For more information on Marion von Osten's research project on such a break in relation to ongoing demands to reform, cf. → http://kunstraum.leuphana.de/projekte/e-reformpause.html (accessed December 29, 2017).
18 Michel Foucault, *Fearless Speech*, ed. Joseph Parson (Los Angeles: Semiotext(e), 2001), 19 f.
19 Louisa Shea speaks of the Cynic as an "aggressive benefactor." Cf. *The Cynic Enlightenment. Diogenes in the Salon* (Baltimore: The Johns Hopkins University Press, 2010), 183.

20 Tiziano Dorandi, ed., *Lives of Eminent Philosophers*, (Cambridge: Cambridge University Press, 2013).

21 In doing so, Foucault follows Karl Marx's suggestion to bind societal changes to changes of the self. Cf. e.g. Marx's third "Thesis on Feuerbach": "The coincidence of the changing of circumstances and of human activity or self-changing can be conceived and rationally understood only as *revolutionary practice*." → https://www.marxists.org/archive/marx/works/1845/theses/theses.htm (accessed December 29, 2017). For the political dimension of the Cynic life according to Foucault, cf. Michael Hardt, "The Militancy of Theory," *South Atlantic Quarterly 110*, no. 1 (2011), 19—35.

22 Louisa Shea blames Peter Sloterdijk for presenting the Cynics as scandalous erotic nature-boys: "Sloterdijk also looked to Diogenes' body as the site of resistance, seeing in the Cynic's predilection for masturbating and defecating in public a comico-grotesque celebration of the primitive, the base, and the socially unacceptable. He discovered in the body's free flow of libidinal energy the explosion of unsocialized 'naturalness' and freedom. This somewhat naive celebration of the intrinsic erotic wholeness of the body contrasts, however, with Foucault's sober articulation of Diogenes' ascetic practices, which provide the Cynic, in Foucault's reading, with the tools necessary to counter the social production of ourselves as 'docile bodies'." Louisa Shea, *The Cynic Enlightenment. Diogenes in the Salon* (Baltimore: The Johns Hopkins University Press, 2010), 180 f.

23 Michel de Certeau, *The Practice of Everyday Life* (Berkeley, Los Angeles, London: University of California Press, 1988), for special practices cf. chapter III.

24 Luc Boltanski and Ève Chiapello, *The New Spirit of Capitalism* (London and New York: Verso, 2005); Jacques Rancière, "The Misadventures of Critical Thought," in *The Emancipated Spectator* (London and New York: Verso, 2009), 25—49.

25 Cf. e.g. Alain Badiou, *Dritter Entwurf eines Manifests für den Affirmationismus* (Berlin: Merve, 2007); Thomas Edlinger, *Der wunde Punkt. Vom Unbehagen an der Kritik* (Frankfurt am Main: Suhrkamp, 2015); Peter Sloterdijk, *Sphären III. Schäume* (Frankfurt am Main: Suhrkamp, 2004), 682. For a critical engagement with such critique of critique, cf. Pascal Jurt, "Gegen die Unfähigkeit in Widersprüchen zu leben. Im Gespräch mit Alex Demirovic und Ruth Sonderegger," in *testcard. Beiträge zur Popgeschichte* #25: Kritik (Mainz: Ventil Verlag, 2017), 216—229.

26 For a more extensive elaboration on this suggestion, cf. Ruth Sonderegger, "Foucaults Kyniker_innen," in Foucaults Gegenwart. Sexualität — Sorge — Revolution, eds. Isabell Lorey, Gundula Ludwig, and Ruth Sonderegger (Vienna: transversal texts, 2016), 47—75, accessed December 28, 2017. → http://transversal.at/books/foucaultsgegenwart.

27 Michel Foucault, "What is Enlightenment?" in *The Foucault Reader*, ed. Paul Rabinow (New York: Pantheon Books, 1984), 50.

Jane Rendell

Silver: A Courthouse Drama

Characters

THE AUSTRALIAN MINING MAGNATE: an Irish man of 47, the model of a colonial pioneer, tall, broadly built, strongly knit, and fair.

THE AUTHOR: a woman of around fifty, with mid-length brown hair and a fringe resting on metal-framed glasses. She wears a grey polo-neck, a tan skirt, and boots. She is tense and slightly distracted, with a vertical frown-line between her eyebrows.

THE BOUNDARY RIDER & PROSPECTOR: a German man in his fifties, with delicate health.

THE CEO: a Scottish man in his early fifties, dressed in a well-cut dark-grey suit, with a well-ironed pale grey shirt and a dove-grey silk tie. His left hand, with short-cut nails, displays a wedding band.

THE PHILOSOPHER: a French man in his early fifties, bald, attractive, dressed in a blue-grey polo-neck, with lightly tanned skin and heavy-framed glasses. He is confident in front of an audience, relaxed and capable of inspiring respect, but not without his critics.

THE REP RISK ANALYST: a Swiss woman in her late thirties, with an expensive haircut, dressed in a formal Swiss business suit, with low-heeled patent shoes. She carries a leather brief case, and in it a copy of a Rep Risk report.

THE YOUNG MAN FROM BENTO RODRIGUES: a Brazilian man in his early twenties, terrified, escaping from the fast-rising toxic flood-waters of a collapsing tailing dam.

THE YOUNG WOMAN OUTSIDE A CORPORATE HEADQUARTERS: a Brazilian woman in her early twenties, angry, in a black T-shirt, with long curly dark hair pulled back from her face.

Positions

THE AUDIENCE: two benches, with THE WITNESS ahead and to the right, THE DEFENDANT ahead and to the left, facing the back of THE POLICE PROSECUTION AND LAWYER, and beyond THE CLERK OF COURT and THE MAGISTRATE.

THE CLERK OF COURT: a wooden chair, on one side of the table in the centre of the courthouse, with THE DEFENDANT to the right, THE WITNESS to the left, facing THE POLICE PROSECUTION AND LAWYER directly, with THE AUDIENCE and the door to the Police Office straight ahead, back to THE MAGISTRATE.

THE DEFENDANT: a box, with THE AUDIENCE to the right, THE MAGISTRATE to the left, facing THE WITNESS directly and, from the side, the faces of THE CLERK OF COURT and THE POLICE PROSECUTION AND LAWYER.

THE MAGISTRATE: a black leather swivel chair, behind a wooden bench, at the back of the courthouse, with THE DEFENDANT to the right, THE WITNESS to the left, facing the back of THE CLERK OF COURT, and, directly, THE POLICE PROSECUTION AND LAWYER, with THE AUDIENCE and the door to the Police Office straight ahead.

THE POLICE PROSECUTION AND LAWYER: a wooden chair, on one side of the table in the center of the courthouse, with THE WITNESS to the right, THE DEFENDANT to the left, facing THE CLERK OF COURT directly and THE MAGISTRATE straight ahead, back to THE AUDIENCE.

THE WITNESS: a box, with THE MAGISTRATE to the right, THE AUDIENCE to the left, facing THE DEFENDANT directly and THE CLERK OF COURT and THE POLICE PROSECUTION AND LAWYER from the side.

Settings

Wilyu-wilyu-yong and The Peaks of the Barrier, Broken Hill, Australia — A Hotel, Northumberland Avenue, London, United Kingdom — An Academic's Office, A London University, United Kingdom — The Mining Memorial, Broken Hill, Australia — The Countryside, Bento Rodrigues, Brazil — Corporate Headquarters, Brazil — The Provost's Dining Room, A London University, United Kingdom — The Courthouse, West Coast Heritage Centre, Zeehan, Tasmania.

Times

• September 1883 • Saturday 26 August 1899 • July 2013 • November 2015 • March 2016 • Saturday 18 March 2017.

Scenes

SCENE 1

"'Pegging Out' Wilyu-wilyu-yong," September 1883, The Peaks of the Barrier, Broken Hill, Australia.

SCENE 2

"The 'Shows' and the 'Deal,'" Saturday 26 August 1899, A Hotel in Northumberland Avenue, London.

SCENE 3

"At Her Desk," July 2013, An Academic's Office, A London University.

SCENE 4

"Between a Rock and a Hard Place," November 2015, The Mining Memorial, Broken Hill.

SCENE 5

"The Countryside Laid Waste," November 2015, Bento Rodriques, Brazil.

SCENE 6

"An Entrance to the Corporate Headquarters," November 2015, Brazil.

SCENE 7

"Ethics Sub-Contracted," March 2016, The Provost's Dining Room. A London University.

* * *

First staged 4—6pm, Saturday 18 March 2017, as one element of *CROCOITE. CROCOITE. SILVER. SILVER/LEAD*, West Coast Heritage Centre, Zeehan, curated by Justy Phillips and Margaret Woodward, for *Sites of Love and Neglect*, curated by Jane Deeth.

SCENE 1

"'Pegging Out' Wilyu-wilyu-yong."

SETTING: Wilyu-wilyu-yong and the Peaks of the Barrier, Broken Hill, September 1883.
AT RISE: All characters are seated among THE AUDIENCE.

(THE AUTHOR, *stands up and announces*)

THE AUTHOR: Scene 1, "'Pegging Out' Wilyu-wilyu-yong," the Peaks of the Barrier, Broken Hill, September 1883.

(THE AUTHOR *walks to sit on* THE CLERK OF COURT*'s chair, and, standing up, says*)

THE AUTHOR: A BOUNDARY RIDER & PROSPECTOR is at the Mount Gipps station, mustering sheep near Broken Hill, on the peaks of the Barrier. The southern portion of the hill, which runs north-east and south-west for 1—2 miles, presents the appearance of a very jagged razor, so fine seems the edge and so peculiar the indications. (*sits*)

(THE BOUNDARY RIDER & PROSPECTOR *rises and walks to stand at the* DEFENDANT*'s box, facing* THE AUDIENCE, *says*)

THE BOUNDARY RIDER & PROSPECTOR: I have discussed with Mr. George McCulloch, the manager and part owner of the station, the promising look of the hill for prospecting, and it has been decided to peg it out in the possibility of discovering a tin lode. "Wilyu-wilyu-yong" the Aboriginal name for Broken Hill, has been applied for in the names of Messrs. George McCulloch, G.A. Lind, and George Urquhart. Seven blocks, or a total of 2 miles, secured along the line of the lode.

(THE AUTHOR *stands*)

THE AUTHOR: Now is the time of silver and the opportunity of the Barrier. It has passed into a proverb amongst dealers that every stock has its turn. Today there will be a run on this, and tomorrow on that scrip. How it is, nobody knows. "It is the fashion." (*sits*)

(BLACKOUT)

(END OF SCENE)

THE AUTHOR and THE BOUNDARY RIDER & PROSPECTOR return to sit among THE AUDIENCE.

SCENE 2

“The ‘Shows’ and the ‘Deal’”

SETTING: A Hotel in Northumberland Avenue, London, Saturday 26 August 1899.
AT RISE: All characters are seated among THE AUDIENCE.

(THE AUTHOR *stands up and announces*)

THE AUTHOR: Scene 2, “The ‘Shows’ and the ‘Deal,’” A Hotel in Northumberland Avenue, London, Saturday 26 August 1899.

(THE AUTHOR *walks to sit on* THE CLERK OF COURT*’s chair, and standing up, says*)

THE AUTHOR: THE AUSTRALIAN MINING MAGNATE is being interviewed for the *Freeman’s Journal* A Hotel in Northumberland Avenue, London, on Saturday 26 August 1899. (*sits*)

(THE AUSTRALIAN MINING MAGNATE rises and walks to stand at the DEFENDANT*’s box, facing* THE AUDIENCE, *says*)

THE AUSTRALIAN MINING MAGNATE: My good fortune came about in this way. In 1889 very encouraging reports came from the Zeehan district of Tasmania of the discovery of high grade galena carrying very rich silver. A friend of mine, Mr. William Orr, induced me to visit the north-west coast, and we became interested together in various prospecting “shows” in the locality which has since been the scene of so much speculation. We subsequently visited it twice a year until about the middle of 1891, when we were offered an interest in what was then known as the Mount Lyell Gold Mining Company, for it is a strange fact that what was to become one of the greatest copper mines in the world has been worked as a gold proposition by a company registered locally and managed from Launceston. Mr. Orr and I decided to look carefully into the business, and in September 1891, we thoroughly inspected the property, and had samples of the various classes of ore, which had been exposed taken. These samples we submitted to Mr. Schlapp, the eminent metallurgist, who was then officially connected with the Broken Hill Proprietary Company, who at once perceived their value and encouraged us to go on with the “deal,” in which, as a matter of fact, he participated. To make a long story short, Mr. Orr, Mr. Schlapp, and I purchased the interest under offer to us on our own terms.

(BLACKOUT)

(END OF SCENE)

THE AUTHOR and THE AUSTRALIAN MINING MAGNATE return to sit among THE AUDIENCE.

SCENE 3
"At Her Desk"

SETTING: An Academic's Office, A London University, July 2013.
AT RISE: All characters are seated among THE AUDIENCE.

(THE AUTHOR *stands up and announces*)

THE AUTHOR: Scene 3, "The Author at Her Desk," an Academic's Office, a London University, July 2013.

(THE AUTHOR *walks to sit on* THE CLERK OF COURT*'s chair; remaining seated and looking down, she whispers anxiously*)

THE AUTHOR: Before dawn, almost every night, I am jolted awake, surprised and disorientated for a second or two, and then I remember, and the panic rears up through me. Will fighting this battle, pitting myself against my institution, lose me my job? Will the right governance structures and due diligence procedures really protect the independence of academic research? Will engaging with businesses really change them? I still don't grasp the logic that, on the one hand, when the funding is at arm's length, the giver of the gift, in this case a mining company, should not influence the activities of the receiver of the gift or be influenced by the activities that the receiver conducts with the funds given, but that, on the other hand, the receiver of the gift, in this case my university, wishes to influence the activities of the giver.

(THE REP RISK ANALYST *walks across to* THE POLICE PROSECUTION*'s chair. She sits down, briskly snaps open her briefcase, takes from it a copy of this script, containing quotes from a Rep Risk report, and, after clearing her throat for effect, starts reading it aloud*)

THE REP RISK ANALYST: The report, *Point of No Return*, published by Greenpeace with research from the environmental consultancy Ecofys, has expressed serious concerns about a boost in mining, oil and gas extraction by major multinational companies, including Adaro Energy, BHP Billiton, Gazprom, Peabody Energy, Vale, and others.

(THE CEO *makes his way in firm swinging strides to* THE DEFENDANT*'s box, and speaks confidently and with feeling*)

THE CEO: We accept the Intergovernmental Panel on Climate Change's (IPCC) assessment of climate change science, which has found that climate warming is unequivocal, the human influence is clear, and the physical impacts are unavoidable.

(THE REP RISK ANALYST *stands up to continue*)

THE REP RISK ANALYST: The report claims that the projected activities of these companies could lead to a 20 per cent increase in CO_2 levels, as well as an increase of 5 to 6 degrees in global temperature by 2020.

(THE CEO, *confidently and with purpose*)

THE CEO: We believe that the world must pursue the twin objectives of limiting climate change to the lower end of the IPCC emission scenarios in line with current international agreements, while providing access to the affordable energy required to continue the economic growth essential for maintaining living standards and alleviating poverty. Under all current plausible scenarios, fossil fuels will continue to be a significant part of the energy mix for decades. There needs to be an acceleration of effort to drive energy efficiency, develop and deploy low emissions technology, and adapt to the impacts of climate change. There should be a price on carbon, implemented in a way that addresses competitiveness concerns and achieves lowest cost emissions reductions.

(THE AUTHOR *looks up, facing* THE REP RISK ANALYST)

THE AUTHOR: When the fear that woke my stomach reached my head, I found myself wide-awake in a still-dark bedroom. I realized that, when the morning came, I would have to outline the research I had conducted for the risk register. I'd been asked to "own" the risk of research expansion, whatever that means (*a slight chuckle*). I have decided to focus on my university's position as a global research leader and remind my colleagues that our academic reputation is based on independence and integrity.

(*facing* THE AUDIENCE)

I am going to suggest that one of the risks associated with research expansion comes from accepting financial gifts from corporations, particularly where there are disparities between the practices of those corporations and our institution's values published as its core principles and procedures.

(*gaining confidence now*)

If we follow the Brundtland Report of 1987, which states that sustainable development must be "development that meets the needs of the present without compromising the ability of future generations to meet their own needs," then fossil fuel mining is unsustainable on two grounds: first, fossil fuels are a finite resource, and second, as the published climate science evidence demonstrates, the limit of the ecosystem to absorb CO_2 has already been dangerously surpassed.

(*leaning forward to emphasize her question*)

How then can a university accept funding from the charitable arm of one of the world's largest mining corporations to set up an Institute of Sustainable Resources?

(THE CEO, *acting as if he has not heard either* THE AUTHOR *or* THE REP RISK ANALYST)

THE CEO: We will continue to take action to reduce our emissions. Build the resilience of our operations, investments, communities, and ecosystems to the impacts of climate change. Recognize our role as policymakers, seek to enhance

the global response by engaging with governments. Work in partnership with resource sector peers to improve sectoral performance and increase industry's influence in policy development to deliver effective long-term regulatory responses. And through material investments in low emissions technology, contribute to reducing emissions from the use of fossil fuels.
(*followed by a deep breath*)

(THE REP RISK ANALYST, *taking advantage of the pause to intervene*)

THE REP RISK ANALYST: The report also argues that the environmental impacts of such changes could lead to impacts on food supplies and a series of social upheavals. Areas of particular concern include coal mining northwestern USA, Indonesia, China and Australia's Gunnedah, Surat and Galilee basins, tar sand exploration and oil pipelines by Enbridge and others in Canada, Arctic drilling by Gazprom and others in Russia, and deep-sea drilling off the Brazilian coast by Petrobras, BP, Shell, Total, and Statoil.

(THE AUTHOR *stands up and walks past* THE CEO, *toward* THE AUDIENCE, *to address them more directly, speaks rather loudly and with authority now*)

THE AUTHOR: In the autumn of 1983, Foucault gave six lectures at the University of California, Berkeley, exploring the practice of *parrhesia* in the Greek culture of the 4th and 5th centuries BC. He examined the evolution of the term with respect to rhetorics, politics, and philosophy, investigating the link between *parrhesia* and the concepts of frankness, truth, danger, criticism, and duty.

(THE PHILOSOPHER *slowly rises and walks across the Courthouse, and up the steps behind* THE MAGISTRATE*'s bench, and, standing, addresses the Courthouse*)

THE PHILOSOPHER: *Parrhesia* is a kind of verbal activity where the speaker has a specific relation to truth through frankness, a certain relationship to his own life through danger, a certain type of relation to himself or other people through criticism (self-criticism or criticism of other people), and a specific relation to moral law through freedom and duty. More precisely, *parrhesia* a speaker expresses his personal relationship to truth and risks his life because he recognizes truth-telling as a duty to improve or help other people (as well as himself).

(BLACKOUT)

(END OF SCENE)

THE AUTHOR, THE REP RISK ANALYST, THE CEO, *and* THE MAGISTRATE *return to sit among* THE AUDIENCE.

SCENE 4

"Between a Rock and a Hard Place"

SETTING: The Mining Memorial, Broken Hill, November 2015.
AT RISE: All characters are seated among THE AUDIENCE.

(THE AUTHOR *stands up and announces*)

THE AUTHOR: Scene 4, "Between a Rock and a Hard Place," The Mining Memorial, Broken Hill, November 2015.

(THE AUTHOR *walks toward* THE CLERK OF COURT*'s chair, and, as she does so, she circles and turns, looks at the ground and mutters to herself*)

THE AUTHOR: And so here she is — finally — her left cheek still hot from the setting sun, squinting to match the hulks of the abandoned mining machinery to the healing tears in the ground, to the lines of the urban grid stretching away into the horizon — Oxide, Chloride, Sulphide, Bromide... She is trying to find the exact spot where it was born. Coming into its orbit has meant drawing a different line, one that has involved a certain refusal and a decision not to comply. The heat, the rough ground underfoot, the scuttle of tails, and the shimmering dust: they all remind me of something way back.

(THE AUTHOR *continues toward* THE CLERK OF COURT*'s chair at the table, pauses and looks up, still talking to herself*)

THE AUTHOR: When she finally gets there, the sun is low in the sky, so low that the rays are almost horizontal.

(*she pauses again*)

I can still feel them now and remember the transforming effect this kind of light, this kind of reflections, could have on me. This is a road of a kind, a surface of hot dry rocks that takes a sharp turn at the bend, in its rise away from one side of the town and toward the other. It is hard to be sure if it was here or there — how does one choose between one rock and another? What can the profile of a rock or a glimmer in the dust tell me of how it all began, and, more importantly, why do I feel the need to look back for the beginnings? Why judge the efforts of these men — according to those men — back then?

(THE AUTHOR *finally reaches* THE CLERK OF COURT*'s chair and sits down. She stares into the space in front of her. Her eyes look from left to right as if she was reading a line of words right in front of her, words that no one else can see*)

THE AUTHOR: Before me, I can see the names of hundreds of dead miners, carefully etched into the thick glass, garlanded with white roses. I can see my own eyes in the reflection, layered over the words: "Vaughn, Master John, 29.07.1886. 14. B.H.P. Mine. Fell Down Ore Heap."

(THE PHILOSOPHER *rises and walks across the courthouse as he approaches* THE AUTHOR, *pauses at her side, and gently taps her on the shoulder. She rises.*)

(THE AUTHOR, *facing the audience directly*)

THE AUTHOR: According to Foucault, the "signature mark" of the critical attitude and its particular virtue is governance: "how not to be governed *like* that, by that, in the name of those principles, with such and such an objective in mind and by means of such procedures, not like that, not for that, not by them."

(THE PHILOSOPHER *continues to walk to the steps leading up to* THE MAGISTRATE*'s bench. He climbs them slowly and lowers himself into the black leather chair, faces the Courthouse, and nods.*)

THE PHILOSOPHER: Just so. Just so.

(*and then very gravely*)

I would therefore propose, as a very first definition of critique, this general characterization: the art of not being governed quite so much.

(BLACKOUT)

(END OF SCENE)

THE AUTHOR and THE PHILOSOPHER return to sit among THE AUDIENCE.

SCENE 5
"The Countryside Laid Waste"

SETTING: Bento Rodrigues, Brazil, November 2015.
AT RISE: All characters are seated among THE AUDIENCE.

(THE AUTHOR *stands up and announces*)

THE AUTHOR: Scene 5, "The Countryside Laid Waste," Bento Rodrigues, Brazil, November 2015. Surrounded by three or four trees, whose bright green foliage stands out, is a rectangular one-storey dwelling, positioned centrally on the stage, but at a diagonal, with a square window (glass missing) in each of the two visible facades. It is covered in a red-brown thick and glossy liquid that spreads out around the house as far as the eye can see. Two cars — one grey, one white — seem to float in it. Another building, located at the back of the stage, has its roof missing. It has collapsed inwards, bringing down a wall. One of the cars appears to be stranded at the corner of an adjacent, also roof-less, building.

(*sits down again among* THE AUDIENCE)

(THE YOUNG MAN FROM BENTO RODRIGUES *stands up and walks across the Courthouse to take up position in* THE WITNESS*'s box. At the same time,* THE CEO *stands up and walks across the Courthouse to take up position in* THE DEFENDANT*'s box.*)

THE YOUNG MAN FROM BENTO RODRIGUES: (*shouting*) Come back Tiago!

THE CEO: (*calmly lifting his left hand to display a wedding band; he holds his hand across his chest so that it rests just above his liver*) I travelled to the region last week, and what I witnessed on site and around the community was truly heart-breaking.

THE YOUNG MAN FROM BENTO RODRIGUES: (*shouting*) The dam is breakin' down, man!

THE CEO: (*calmly*) We are deeply sorry to everyone who has and will suffer from this terrible tragedy.

THE YOUNG MAN FROM BENTO RODRIGUES: (*shouting*) Go, Tiago, go faster!

THE CEO: (*calmly*) We want this Fund to assist the affected families and communities as quickly as possible.

THE YOUNG MAN FROM BENTO RODRIGUES: (*shouting*) Look at the truck...

THE CEO: (*calmly*) We are determined to bring together all of the necessary skill, experience and expertise this ongoing effort will require, and we will learn the lessons to improve all our operations.

THE YOUNG MAN FROM BENTO RODRIGUES: (*shouting*) Go back, go back, go back, go back!

THE CEO: (*calmly*) I would also like to thank people here in Australia and in the UK for their messages of support. My family and I are enormously grateful.

THE YOUNG MAN FROM BENTO RODRIGUES: (*shouting*) Oh man, turn back the truck, and let's get away from here!

THE CEO: (*calmly*) Thank you from the bottom of my heart.

THE YOUNG MAN FROM BENTO RODRIGUES: (*shouting*) Come back André! Let's get out of here!

THE CEO: (*calmly*) At every stage we will continue to be guided by our Charter Values. Our Charter enshrines the values of Sustainability, Integrity, Respect, Performance, Simplicity, and Accountability. It defines who we are and what we stand for as an organisation.

THE YOUNG MAN FROM BENTO RODRIGUES: (*shouting*) It killed the guys, man!

THE CEO: (*calmly*) Our first Charter Value of Sustainability is our commitment to Health and Safety. So the tragedy in Brazil goes to the very heart of who we are as a company.

THE YOUNG MAN FROM BENTO RODRIGUES: (*screaming now*) It killed everyone, man! Holy Mother...

(BLACKOUT)

(END OF SCENE)

THE CEO and THE YOUNG MAN FROM BENTO RODRIGUES return to sit among THE AUDIENCE.

SCENE 6
"The Entrance to the Corporate Headquarters"

SETTING: Brazil, November 2015.
AT RISE: All characters are seated among THE AUDIENCE.

(THE AUTHOR *stands up and announces*)

THE AUTHOR: Scene 6, "The Entrance to the Corporate Headquarters," Brazil, November 2015. A marble-clad column is located at the front of the corporate headquarters. A woman in a black t-shirt steps forward, her black curly hair pulled back from her face. She raises one arm, her hand covered in mud, and starts smearing it across the marble, working it back and forth across the shiny surface. Then she lifts up a plastic tub and throws the remainder hard so that it splatters right across the company's logo and letters, raised in profile.

(*sits down again among* THE AUDIENCE)

(THE YOUNG WOMAN OUTSIDE THE CORPORATE HEADQUARTERS *stands up and walks across the Courthouse to take up position in* THE WITNESS*'s box. At the same time,* THE REP RISK ANALYST *stands up and walks across the Courthouse to take up position in the* THE POLICE PROSECUTION & LAWYER*'s chair.*)

THE YOUNG WOMAN OUTSIDE THE CORPORATE HEADQUARTERS: (*chanting*) No! It was no accident! No!

THE REP RISK ANALYST: (*reading from the script on the desk in front of her*) Brazilian police have requested for the arrest of Samarco's chief executive and six others after having been charged with homicide linked to the collapse of the miner's dam in November 2015. They have also been accused of endangering public health after the collapse of the dam [Note of Rep Risk Analyst: refers to the Fundao Tailings dam, which is part of the Germano mine], which spewed mining waste and polluted drinking water. Reports claim that the incident, which was considered by the government to be Brazil's worst environmental disaster, led to the death of 17 people, buried communities, and displaced a total of 725 people. The incident has also resulted in several legal cases including a USD 5.1 billion lawsuit by Brazil's attorney general, state and federal prosecutor lawsuits demanding compensation to damages, as well a plea to freeze BRL 500 million of Samarco's assets to guarantee town repairs. Samarco is a joint venture between Vale and BHP Billiton.

THE YOUNG WOMAN OUTSIDE THE CORPORATE HEADQUARTERS: (*chanting*) No! It was no accident! No!

THE REP RISK ANALYST: (*continuing to read from the script on the desk in front of her*) A court in the Brazilian state of Minas Gerais has ordered the freezing of BRL 500 million owned by Samarco, Vale, and BHP Billiton for the environmental damage caused by the collapse of the Fundao dam in Mariana, Brazil. The order follows a request from the State Public Ministry. The funds will be used to compensate for damaged or destroyed infrastructure, buildings, sewage systems, and water supply systems for schools, public spaces, and football fields. The mining companies have been asked to carry out containment works on the Carmo river in order to avoid landslides and to guarantee the stability of the river banks. The judge also ordered the companies to establish evacuation and alert plans in the case of further disasters. The companies have also been asked to provide a 6-month recovery plan within the next 30 days, and risk facing daily fines of BRL 500,000 if they do not submit the plan on time.

THE YOUNG WOMAN OUTSIDE THE CORPORATE HEADQUARTERS: (*chanting*) No! It was no accident! No!

(BLACKOUT)

(END OF SCENE)

THE REP RISK ANALYST and THE YOUNG WOMAN OUTSIDE THE CORPORATE HEADQUARTERS return to sit among THE AUDIENCE.

SCENE 7
"Ethics Sub-Contracted"

SETTING: The Provost's Dining Room, A London University, March 2016.
AT RISE: All characters are seated among THE AUDIENCE.

(THE AUTHOR *stands up and announces*)

THE AUTHOR: Scene 7, "Ethics Sub-contracted," The Provost's Dining Room, A London University, March 2016. Tucked away at the top of a strange dog-legged staircase, the Provost's Dining Room is just large enough to hold a table for an intimate dinner for six. She has to call the Security Guard to find it.

(THE AUTHOR *walks to sit in* THE CLERK OF COURT*'s chair.* THE PHILOSOPHER *slowly rises and walks across the Courthouse, and up the steps behind* THE MAGISTRATE*'s bench, and, standing, addresses the Courthouse.*)

THE PHILOSOPHER: Here, giving an account of your life, your bios, is also not to give a narrative of the historical events that have taken place in your life, ...

THE AUTHOR: (*seated, with her back to* THE MAGISTRATE) I had to call a security guard to find the room. It was empty of the committee when I arrived. But the secretary was already there, pouring coffee and adding finishing touches to the paper work.

THE PHILOSOPHER: (*continuing*) ...but rather to demonstrate whether you are able to show that there is a relation between the rational discourse, the logos you are able to use, and the way that you live.

THE AUTHOR: (*rising now, but still with her back to* THE MAGISTRATE) In the future, it seems as if it has been decided that it will no longer be necessary for academics to be involved in making decisions that concern ethical investments. Instead, the work is to be sub-contracted.

THE PHILOSOPHER: (*continuing*) Socrates is inquiring into the way that logos gives form to a person's style of life...

THE AUTHOR: (*turning to face* THE MAGISTRATE) It strikes me that this is a convenient way to avoid the potential and actual offense to investors that might be caused by divesting from specific fossil fuel companies.

All characters sitting among THE AUDIENCE: (*eyebrows raised, with quizzical expressions*) And what of you, who chose, and still chooses, to fly?

THE PHILOSOPHER: (*frowning a little at the unexpected interruption, and then continuing*) For he (*and then adding, with a dazzling smile*) or, of course, she (*and concluding*) is interested in discovering whether there is a harmonic relation between the two.

(BLACKOUT)

(THE END)

This script is a piece of experimental writing that has been composed using found sources to create speech for a number of invented characters, given in CAPS, extracted from the following references:

"The Barrier Silver Field and Tin Fields in 1888," a series of letters written by a special correspondent of *The South Australian Register*, *Adelaide Oserver*, and *Evening Journal*, and reprinted from those papers (Adelaide: W. K. Thomas & Co., 1888). See the words of THE BOUNDARY RIDER AND PROSPECTOR.

"Mr Bowes Kelly. An Australian Mining King. His Big Interest in Broken Hill and Mount Lyell." *Freeman's Journal*, Sydney (Saturday, 26 August 1899): 24. See the words of THE AUSTRALIAN MINING MAGNATE.

"Point of No Return. The massive climate threats we must avoid." *Greenpeace International*, 22 January, 2013. → http://www.greenpeace.org/international/en/publications/Campaign-reports/Climate-Reports/Point-of-No-Return (accessed 16 February 2017). See the words of THE REP RISK ANALYST.

Michel Foucault, "Discourse and Truth: The Problematization of Parrhesia." Six lectures given by Foucault at the University of California at Berkeley from October-November 1983. → http://foucault.info/system/files/pdfDiscourseAndTruth_MichelFoucault_1983_0.pdf, (accessed 16 February 2017). See the words of THE PHILOSOPHER.

Michel Foucault, "What Is Critique?," in *The Politics of Truth*. (New York: Semiotext(e), 2007), 41—82. See the words of THE PHILOSOPHER.

"Rep Risk Company Report, *BHP Billiton PLC*" (also listed as *BHP Billiton Ltd*), Tuesday 28 May 2013. See the words of THE REP RISK ANALYST.

"Rep Risk Company Report, *BHP Billiton Group*" (*BHP Billiton*), Thursday 21 April 2016. See the words of THE REP RISK ANALYST.

"Speech by *BHP Billiton*'s CEO Andrew McKenzie, at The Annual General Meeting of *BHP Billiton Limited*, 10.00 a.m. (Perth time), Thursday, 19 November 2015 at the Perth Convention and Exhibition Centre, Perth, Western Australia." → https://www.youtube.com/watch?v=JxFq1w2X7VE (accessed 16 February 2017). See the words of THE CEO.

Matthew Stevens, "*BHP Billiton*'s Andrew Mackenzie Weeps as Dam Disaster Toll Mounts." *Financial Review*, Nov. 20 2015. → http://www.afr.com/business/mining/bhp-billitons-andrew-mackenzie-weeps-as-dam-disaster-toll-mounts-20151119-gl32sm#ixzz4BYRxZ1PM (accessed 16 February 2017). See the words of THE CEO.

Marcelo Bicharo, "The Valley of the Dead River," 2016. → https://www.youtube.com/watch?v=mAPn5zVN56Q (accessed 16 February 2017). See the words of THE YOUNG MAN FROM BENTO RODRIGUES and THE YOUNG WOMAN OUTSIDE THE CORPORATE HEADQUARTERS.

Jane Rendell, "Giving An Account Of Oneself, Architecturally Architecture!," edited by Jae Emerling and Ronna Gardner, Special Issue of the *Journal of Visual Culture 15*, no. 3, 2016, 334—348. See the words of THE AUTHOR.

fig. 2 Saydnaya prison, as reconstructed by Forensic Architecture using architectural and acoustic modelling.

Eyal Weizman
Michael Klein and Christina Linortner

The Fragility of Truth: An Interview with Forensic Architecture

Forensic Architecture is a multidisciplinary research agency based at Goldsmiths, University of London, that operates as a counter-forensic agency. It investigates cases of human rights violations by states and corporations, and of state violence by means of architectural knowledge and techniques. In order to do so, a multidisciplinary team of architects and filmmakers, coders, investigative journalists, lawyers, and scientists provide evidence files for the media, for investigative platforms (like *The Intercept*), and for tribunals, courts, human rights reports, and art events. In 2017, Forensic Architecture conducted a counter-investigation concerning the testimony of a German secret service agent in the case of the racist murder of Halit Yogzat, carried out by the National Socialist Underground (NSU) in Kassel in 2006. The results of the investigation, which involved physical and digital experiments, were ultimately referenced in the NSU trial.

Forensic Architecture's director Eyal Weizman (EW) in conversation with Michael Klein (MK) and Christina Linortner (CL).

CL As an agency, you use the term “Forensic Architecture,” but you describe what you do as a *counter-forensic* practice. What is the role of forensics in your work?

EW Forensics is what states do. Forensics is the way the police works in order to survey and sometimes control the population. *Counter-forensics*, is, however, returning to the forensic case — this is what the civil society organizations do when they face repressive regimes. It is an inversion of the forensic gaze: investigating the investigators, taking over the means of production, in the sense of taking over the means of epistemic or knowledge production. The term *counter-forensics* has been coined by Allan Sekula in the work he did when digging for the disappeared in Kurdistan. We found it useful. And this is how we use it.

MK So could we understand *counter-forensics* as the critical project of forensics?

EW Forensic Architecture obviously relies on the impetus in politics, visual practices, and visual theory, but it differs from critique.

MK In what sense does it differ? Do you consider Forensic Architecture along one of the many lines of the critical project, like that of enlightenment — or wherever you want it to come from? Is it led by the impetus of critical theory or related approaches? Where would you position your practice?

EW A lot of us are theorists. In my previous work, I wrote within the critical mode. The investigative mode, however, is slightly different. The critical mode assumes a surface-and-depth model of culture and politics. Symptoms on the surface are mere representations of massive formative forces in the depth. If you were a psychoanalyst, it would be the sub-conscious that shows symptoms on the surface. If you were a Nietzschean scholar, it would be the will for power. If you were a Marxist, it would be the class struggle, the formative forces that in a modernist critical conception needed to be discovered behind layers of representation, whereas representations operate also as tiles of broken mirrors of distortion.

Our work is based on a certain suspicion toward representation, based on the idea of fundamental truths that need to be unearthed. The critical scholar is like a whale hunter who sends the harpoon into the depth, piercing those layers of representations in order to capture the truthful essence of situations. Our relation to truth is very different, it is something that we understand as fragile, as something that needs to be composed, that needs to be defended, that needs to be assembled. The investigative impetus is also one of building and constructing.

So in *counter-forensics* there are usually two moves. One is to debunk the official truths, the narratives of the police, the narratives of the state, of the military, and of the people who think they have the monopoly of representation in order to show the contradictions, to show the weak points within that narrative, to show where it fails, being critical is useful for that purpose. On the other hand, when needing to piece together something else, you need to construct it in a way that it is strong enough to face counter attacks. In our model, truth is always a product of conflict, and this is where we come into action. So, for instance, in the Kassel case, you would have a faint shadow of failure, of an institutional failure of the state's cover-up that is cast upon the entire NSU case, which shows the presence of a secret service agent over the surface in Kassel. All we are trying to do in this investigation is to show that the person is lying. But the aim is to ask much more fundamental and larger questions about the way in which the German society is dealing with migration, the way in which the police and the judiciary might be polluting, marginalizing, and terrorizing migrant populations, and other such things. So we start with a point of irregularity, and then try to make a crack that would travel through and cut through much larger political structures, thus revealing in it the history. And this is somehow the essence of Forensic Architecture's work. You start from a micro-event, from an instance, and you try to arrive at the *longue durée* of historical courses. So you are saying: within that internet shop in Kassel, all the actors that compose the NSU complex are architecturally disposed in relation to each other: the state representative, the killers, and the migrant communities that are being targeted. You see those bigger forces colliding at the shop. You also see how this is the story of many things to do — with Germany's history, with Germany's unification, with the migration of the policing practices from the Eastern (GDR) security service to the Bundesrepublik security service, with the imaginary of a deep state that might come from the Turkish activists working on this case, etc. So there is always more than you can see in these little micro-events.

CL Forensic Architecture works in many different places around the world, like Palestine, Mexico, Syria, or Germany—what kind of background knowledge is involved in this work?

EW We would always work on behalf of and together with communities that feel threatened by repressive governments, and we would tie our work into the existing civil society-led political processes, so it is not simply a kind of tactical scientific evidence that just floats there in the ether, but it is networked onto the ground. It is through them that we learn about those conflicts and tie those micro-events to the larger history.

CL You mentioned certain findings that are revealed through your process: things you uncover, like the consequences of merging two different policing systems the unified Germany. Do you already know about such particular circumstances beforehand, or is this all the knowledge you gain through the process?

EW These are all kinds of reflections that come out of a slow and long work process or relations with people on the ground.

MK Unlike much traditional critique, which is merely based on words, your argument, your explanation almost always involves other sources, other forms of evidence, building on cartography, modeling, or re-enactments. It is as if objects and material—or matter, in general—spoke for itself and told a story. For a major part of the 20th century, witness testimonies were crucial in the critique and struggle of the civil society against, for instance, totalitarianism. In the practice of Forensic Architecture, there seems to be an attempt of bringing matter to speaking the truth—Susan Schuppli once proposed the term *material witness*.[1] It builds, however, on a very different episteme than the human witness. What is the relationship between matter speaking for itself and the human witness?

EW I do not believe in a separation like that. The project began with a certain reflection on the forensic term on

fig. 3 Composite of Forensic Architecture's physical and virtual reconstructions of the internet cafe in which the murder of Halit Yozgat on 6 April 2006 occurred.

fig. 4 Simulated propagation of sound within a digital model of the internet cafe that was designed to mimic the exact dimensions and materials of the actual space.

the shifting away from subject-based epistemologies to object-based epistemologies within human rights, but we are always very critical of that. In our work, we are very much trying to combine them in order to say that while evidence is the category that relates to objects and testimony is the category that relates to subjects, they need to be blurred. The difference needs to be blurred and entangled. In our legal work, we always do blur them, so, for instance, evidence is used in order to instigate new testimonies, or we build our architectural models with witnesses, like in the Saydnaya project,[2] as doorways into memory — so that they remember. Evidence operates on the memory because it triggers things that are connected to particular events, and, likewise, some evidence is the product of memory description — again, what comes to mind is the models that we build with witnesses. We try to understand exactly this subject-object relation through a set of production that does not separate them but entangles them further, that places the witness in an embedded position. Or, let's put it like that: There is no object that speaks for itself. Objects speak through people, objects speak through an expert who ventriloquizes them or channels information that comes from a material investigation into the forum. The forum itself is a space of speech, so indeed we work with images, with materials, with models and memory, but language is a part of it. There is no pure matter that exists before language — this is not some kind of Paleolithic archaeology, where you would only see matter and have no language traces of humanity. This way you can only look at archaeology as a purely material practice without language. There is always language. When we analyze videos from war-zones, they are always images of something that has happened and then, simultaneously, there is a comment, a language-based comment, narration that is spoken over those images because anyone rarely records something, a video, without speaking. So whenever they see something, people often also speak over their videos, or breathe or cry or other things.

MK What can architecture, architectural tools or knowledge, provide in the undertaking of an investigation such as crimes against human rights?

EW Firstly, most violence takes place in cities, and most people that die now in wars die inside buildings. Therefore, it is very important to introduce new forms of knowledge, yet architecture operates on different levels: as a material sensor in as much as the transformation of the materiality of architecture registers events around themselves like contemporary archaeology. Then it operates as a way of synthesizing media: building architectural models, for example, allows placing in space and time all the sources that you can find as representations of particular events in order to synthesize and navigate between them. Or you could use architecture as a mnemonic device that is a gateway to recollection. By building architectural models, witnesses remember things that they might otherwise forget. So architecture precisely links subjects, objects, and media — material evidence — as an object, recollection — as a subject, and media — as social media. It synthesizes what we call the architectural image complex, i.e. a way of navigating between images rather than editing them in a montage sort of way.

CL You described the work of Forensic Architecture like a detective agency, bringing together and assembling the pieces. And like a detective agency, moreover, you said you are commissioned by clients. How do you choose among inquiries? Are there any limits as to whom you would work for? Are there any rules?

EW You are right. We do not take commissions from states. We only work for civil society. We always work for victims. Although that is a category that is often contested: who is the victim in a particular situation? We always work for the universal principles of human rights or solidarity among people. And we choose the cases that we can add most value to as architects, in a sense that we know we would make a difference.

CL You relate the term *forensis* also to its Latin origin and its initial meaning of "belonging to the forum," the public. What is the audience that Forensic Architecture addresses? There is definitely an architecture-arts aspect to your work, which you also show in the context of the art world, like biennials or the documenta. But then you also collaborate with NGOs defending human rights.

EW In the field of counter-forensics, you do not have an organized set of forums: you do not have the courts pre-existing with their own protocols. So we always need to find new forums for explaining, debating, and politically arguing for our work, and we need to move in between different audiences and institutional contexts: from academic institutions, to public institutions, to activist institutions, to the community-based work, to legal forums in courts, and otherwise. That is what is very important for our work.

MK And this is also the reason why you show it in an art context?

EW We always need to find a place to address the audience. And it is just one of the forums in which we do this. But the arts discourse and the visual cultures are very important to us because they are attuned to accentuating and decoding the perceptible. For many years, visual culture was dedicated to decoding the visual world, but, of course, we also work with the auditory and other senses. So there is a lot that could also be learned. It is not only an opportunity to address an audience and to put it there, but, at its best, the arts context is a very robust intellectual engagement with the sensible.

1 → http://susanschuppli.com/research/materialwitness

2 Forensic Architecture and Amnesty International worked together on the case of the Saydnaya Prison in Syria. → https://saydnaya.amnesty.org

Nina Kolowratnik
Johannes Pointl

Mapping Demands for an Architecture of Hospitality

This essay argues for the need to resist the current asylum system in Austria and proposes the introduction of architectural mapping into the discourse of hospitality towards refugees. Mapping is here understood both as a tool to question the existing spatial and political conditions and as an instrument to imagine and demand alternative scenarios of arrival. In Austria, the geographically isolated location of a large number of asylum seeker accommodations[1] limits the opportunities to establish social networks and participate actively in society. The possibility for refugees to act politically is undermined by their absence in the public sphere. Currently, refugees have no right to choose either the type or the location of their accommodation. There are no legally binding spatial standards for asylum seeker accommodations, and it is left up to the benevolence of private operators of accommodations to provide a space that would offer both physical and mental refuge and that the refugees could identify with. Because the shortage of opportunities to take control of their own lives is often a major reason why refugees flee from their countries of origin in the first place, it is all the more necessary to facilitate self-organization at their places of arrival so that they are not, once again, pushed into a state of social and political paralysis. The on-going research and teaching project “Fluchtraum Österreich”[2] positions itself as a form of resistance against the diverse manifestations of borders and the conditions of confinement that characterize the built spaces that refugees are confronted with upon arriving in Austria. The process of mapping aims to provoke a discussion on the spatial desires and claims of refugees in Austria and to provide tools to work towards better conditions of arrival.

1. Refugee Protest

In 2012, the Refugee Protest Camp Vienna marked the first self-organized political movement of refugees in Austria with the aim to instigate a public conversation about the human rights of refugees in the European Union. The protest formed in Austria’s initial reception centre in the town of Traiskirchen. After a 25km long protest march to the city centre of Vienna, the demonstration culminated in the set-up of a permanent protest camp in the public Votiv park along Vienna’s central boulevard Ringstraße. At the core of the protest stood demands for the “right to stay” and better living conditions.[3]

The Refugee Protest Camp Vienna stands for a collective action by refugees to manifest themselves within the public both spatially and discursively. While the protests took place in Austria, Germany, Denmark, Turkey, Bulgaria, Greece, France, and the Netherlands in 2012, these events remain a rare instance of self-organization and pronounced resistance from within the refugee community. That the refugees in Austria rarely enter the political arena can be traced back to two phenomena. The first one is the limiting public perception of refugees as apolitical subjects fuelled by the adoption of the vocabulary of bureaucracy and legal frameworks that the asylum system puts forward. In the Austrian public discourse, the refugees are represented solely as a part of the asylum system, the system that provides them with special ID cards, limits their range of movement, dictates their place of residence, and controls their daily routine. *Birgit Miksch's mapping "Institution of Asylum Austria" (fig. 5) visualizes the rules and processes of the Austrian asylum system in a fictional building. Her choice of pairing a set of architectural elements with the set of steps refugees have to take in Austria reveals the variety of obstacles that they experience as a part of the asylum process. The mapping proposes a critical reading of the existing asylum system and creates a basis for discussions about the redesign of the existing asylum policies.*

The second aspect that hinders refugees from becoming politically emancipated actors in Austria directly relates to space, resulting from the geographic decentralization of most refugee accommodations. This decentralization dates back to the first organized accommodation of asylum seekers by the Austrian government in November 1956, when 170,000 Hungarians who fled their country during the Hungarian Uprising and arrived in Eastern Austria. According to political scientist Raimund Pehm, the distribution of newcomers across the countryside in small-scale tourist establishments and private accommodations located in towns and villages was an attempt to prevent the formation of a Hungarian resistance movement-in-exile during the Cold War.[4] The strategic advantages that the decentralized and small-scale nature of asylum seeker accommodations provides for the Austrian asylum regime have been exploited up until today. That such accommodations are spread across the entire country, often in remote locations, leads to an organized disintegration of refugees[5] that hinders their social inclusion *fig.* 5 Birgit Miksch — "Institution of Asylum Austria"

SEQUENCE OF STATIONS

1 Application for International Protection
2 Data acquisition
3 Photographs
4 Fingerprints
5 Baggage screening
6 Initial Reception Center Traiskrichen
7 Initial Reception Center Thalham
8 Medical examination
9 First interrogation
10 Legal advice from NGOs
11 Second interrogation
12 Exit area for green identity card
13 Administrative decision on application for International Protection
14 Complaint with Federal Administrative Court

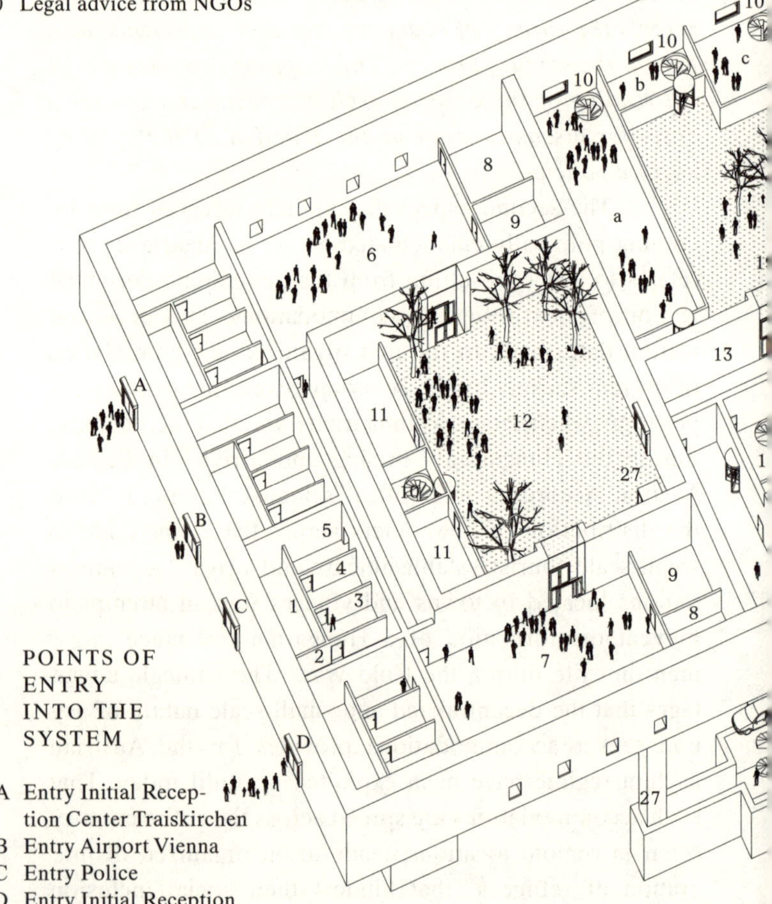

POINTS OF ENTRY INTO THE SYSTEM

A Entry Initial Reception Center Traiskirchen
B Entry Airport Vienna
C Entry Police
D Entry Initial Reception Center Thalham

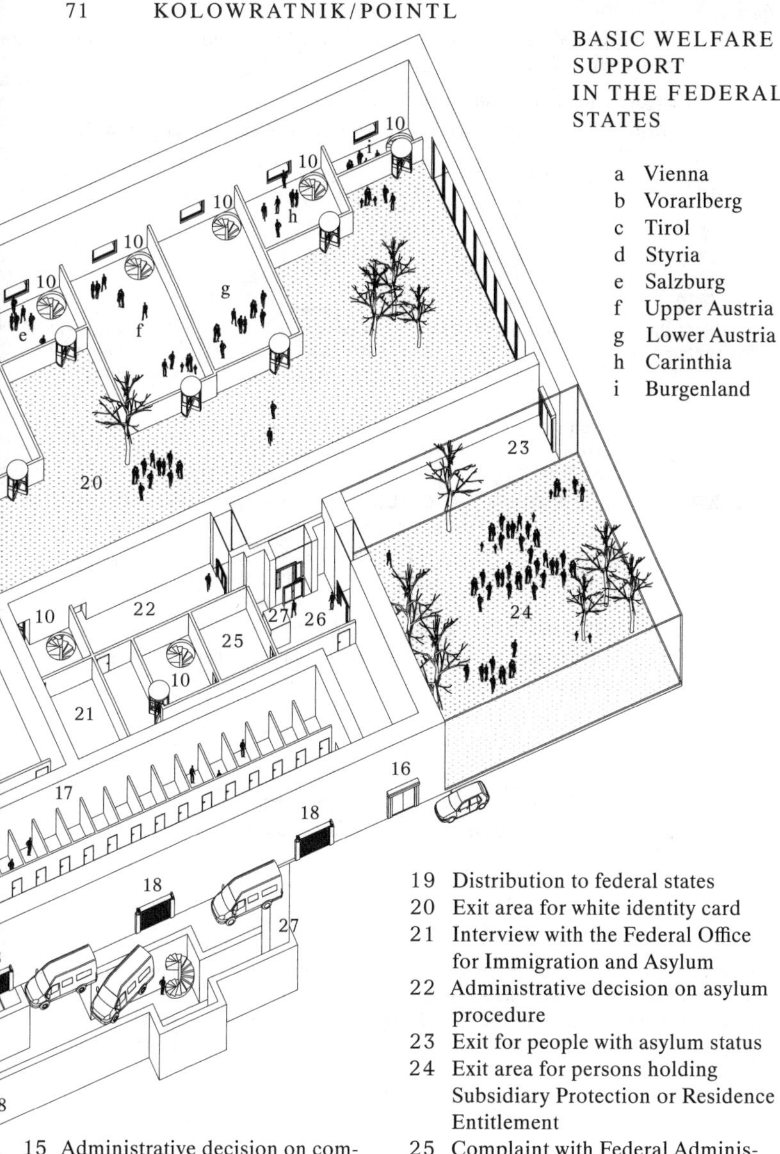

15 Administrative decision on complaints concerning admission procedure
16 "Voluntary Return"
17 Custody to secure deportation
18 Deportation
19 Distribution to federal states
20 Exit area for white identity card
21 Interview with the Federal Office for Immigration and Asylum
22 Administrative decision on asylum procedure
23 Exit for people with asylum status
24 Exit area for persons holding Subsidiary Protection or Residence Entitlement
25 Complaint with Federal Administrative Court and retrial
26 Administrative decision by Federal Administrative Court
27 Renewed asylum procedure
28 Level of NGOs

ad fig. 5

PEOPLE — Frequentation of stations, points of congestion and waiting

ROOM SIZE — Duration of stay in the statio

WALLS — Limitation and barrier to the environment

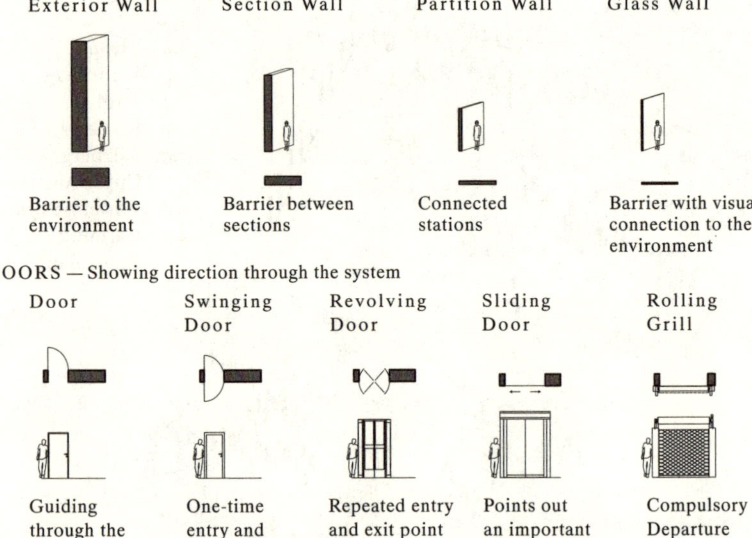

Exterior Wall — Barrier to the environment

Section Wall — Barrier between sections

Partition Wall — Connected stations

Glass Wall — Barrier with visual connection to the environment

DOORS — Showing direction through the system

Door — Guiding through the system

Swinging Door — One-time entry and exit point

Revolving Door — Repeated entry and exit point

Sliding Door — Points out an important stage

Rolling Grill — Compulsory Departure

WINDOWS

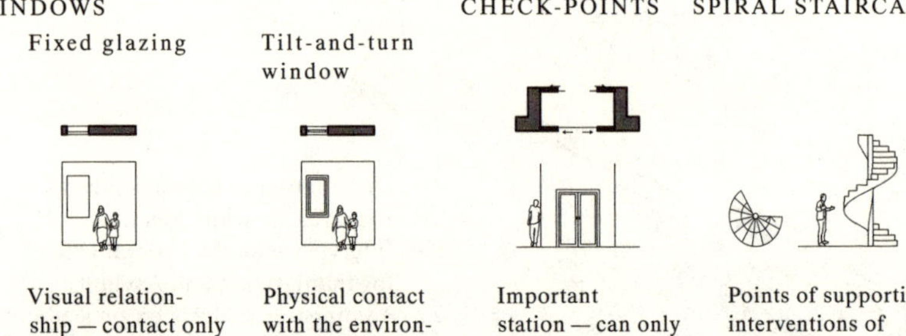

Fixed glazing — Visual relationship — contact only to a limited extent

Tilt-and-turn window — Physical contact with the environment to a limited extent

CHECK-POINTS — Important station — can only be crossed with an administrative decree

SPIRAL STAIRCASES — Points of supportive interventions of NGOs within the system

COURTYARDS — limited freedom within the system

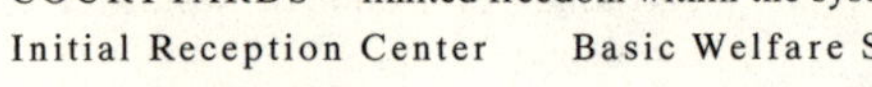

Initial Reception Center

With the green identity card leaving the IRC is allowed but the movement is restricted to the district level.

Basic Welfare Support

With the white identity card full mobility within Austria is granted but leaving the country is prohibited.

Subsidiary Protection and Residence Entitlemen

Full mobility within Austria is granted also leaving the count People holding SP cannot travel to their home country.

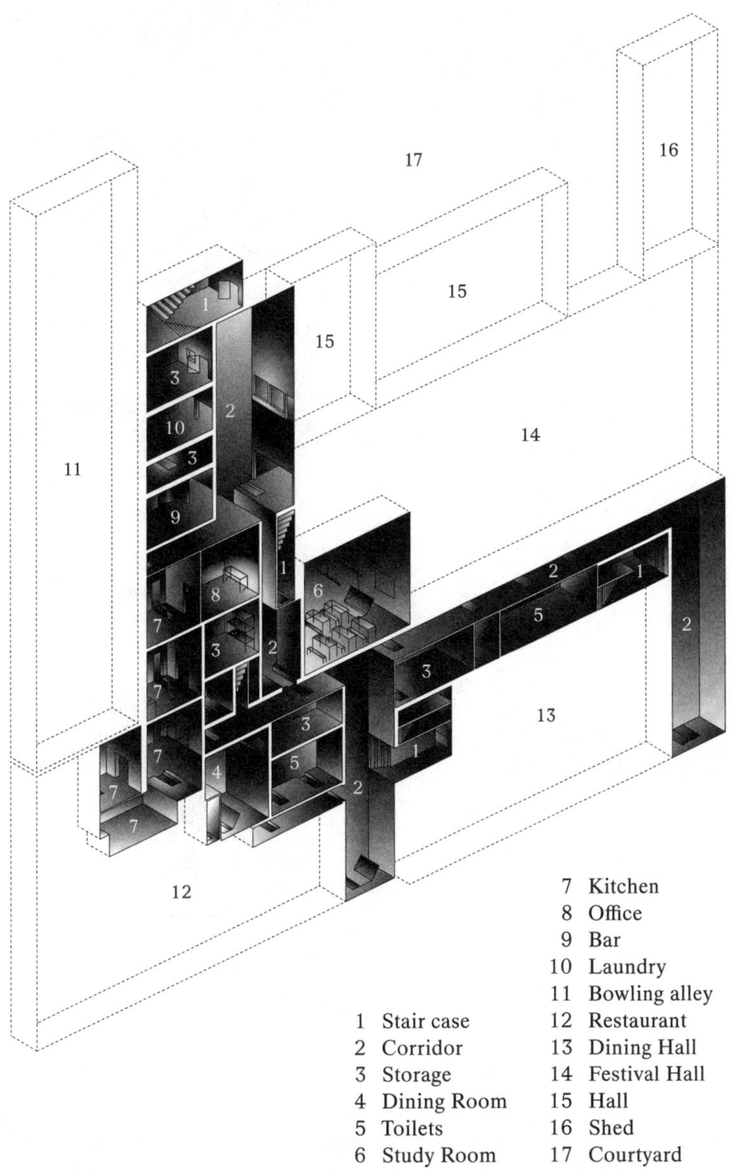

fig. 6 Johannes Puchleitner—"Dead Spaces"

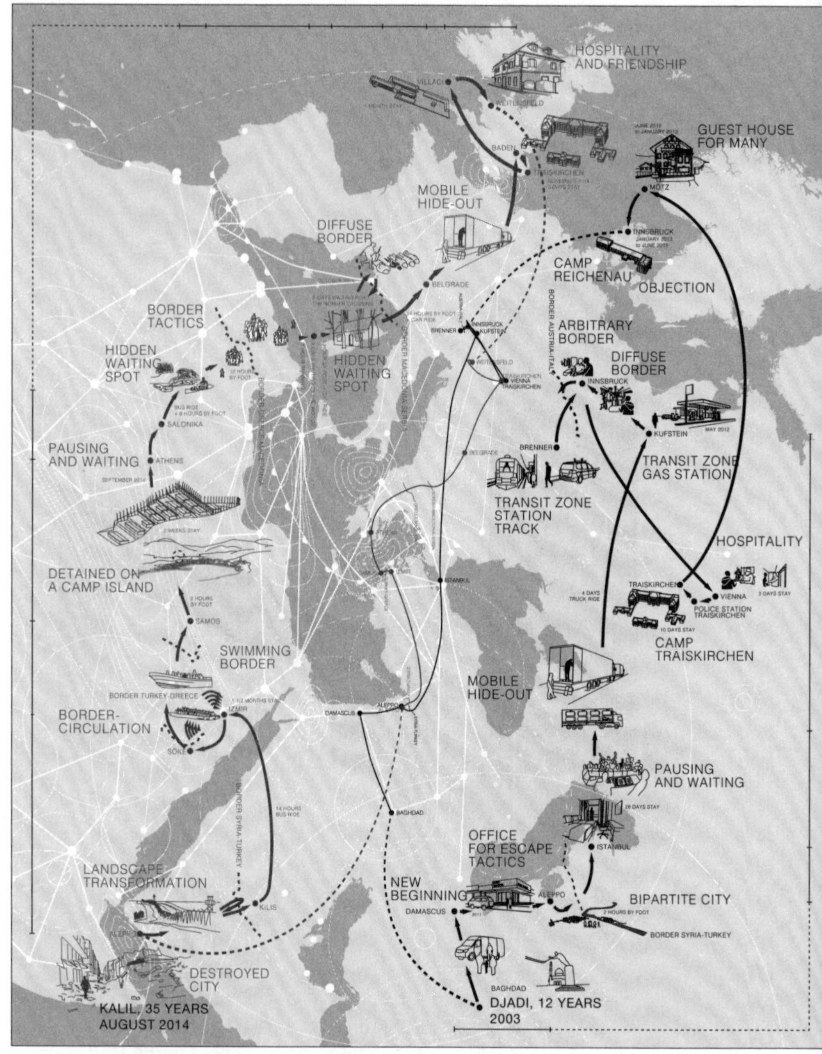

fig. 7 Anton Wagner and Mario Weisböck — "Borders and Movement"

KALIL, 35 Years, Aleppo, DJADI, 24 Years, Baghdad, Major connecting/connecting/Minor connecting routes, Minor/Major Airports, Minor/Major coastal migration hubs, Trucks/cars used as means of transportation, Country of origin, Country of asylum, IDPs — last three: as of midyear 2014, High risk zones, Frontex Joint and limits their opportunities to act politically. *Johannes Puchleitner's mapping "Dead Spaces" (fig. 6) highlights the correlation between the major refugee movements and the incremental investments in the built structure of small-scale accommodations since the 1950s. In this example, the absurdly high number of additions to the ground floor of an existing building located at the Austrian-Hungarian border resulted in a labyrinth of rooms and corridors without daylight and with very limited usability. The mapping questions the minimum standards for common spaces in the accommodations for asylum seekers and aims to instigate a discussion on the spatial resources of former tourism facilities and their potential to benefit the needs of asylum seekers, as well as local residents.*

2. Spaces of Asylum as a Field of Activity for the Spatial Practitioner

The role of the architect in the process of the decentralization and depoliticization of refugees is often one of an unwitting accomplice of an asylum system that tries to limit self-determination and movement. Design proposals and design-build projects emerge and disappear globally along with the fluctuations of refugee movements. These interventions tackle almost exclusively the immediate needs of providing shelter and improving inhuman living conditions within the framework dictated by asylum regimes — in most cases without critiquing the system as such. The question arises whether architectural practitioners must resort to mitigating the state of exception and simply react to the given circumstances with emergency architecture, or whether we can think of a critical understanding of the discipline that goes beyond highlighting, reporting, and up-

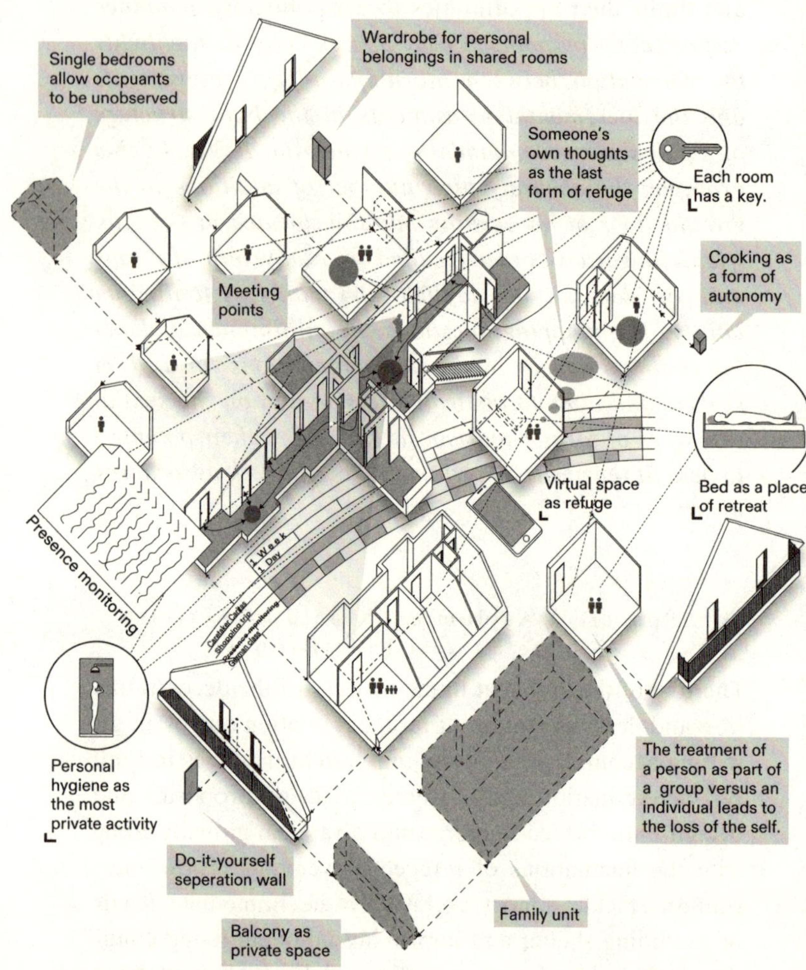

fig. 8 Enrico Weiser — “Places of Retreat”

grading the socio-spatial aspects of asylum and would increasingly participate actively in the political discourse.

The research and teaching project "Fluchtraum Österreich" calls attention to the effects of spatial action and planning on the state of refuge and, it argues for a proactive inclusion of architecture in the asylum discourse. It aims to identify and resist the multiple manifestations of borders and conditions of confinement that refugees currently face in Austria. *Anton Wagner and Mario Weisböck's mapping "Borders and Movement" (fig. 7) addresses the spatial and temporal mutability of borders that two refugees crossed on their way from the Middle East to Austria by juxtaposing the official data sets of the European border control agencies and the refugees' individual experience of the border zones.*

By employing architectural mapping, asylum spaces are questioned on different scales, the largest one being the organization of the current asylum system and its spatial ramifications. The smallest scale represents the immediate environment of refugees that, in most cases, is reduced to a space of mere staying in contrast to a proper place of living. There is a direct correlation between the living quality of refugees and the political framework in Austria. There are no legally determined minimum standards for asylum seeker accommodations, and proprietors can only orient themselves using extremely vaguely defined guidelines. In the absence of spatial accommodation standards, refugees have to resort to small-scale spatial tactics for maintaining or regaining their privacy. *Enrico Weiser's mapping "Places of Retreat" (fig. 8) analyzes how important it is for refugees to be able to construct their personal spaces within accommodations that force them to share kitchens, bathrooms, and bedrooms with complete strangers for several weeks or months. Retreating into virtual space is as important as to resorting to spatial tactics for the appropriation of the immediate living environment, mostly practiced on the scale of the individual room or furniture.*

3. Mapping Demands

Within the "Fluchtraum Österreich" project, one of the strategies to oppose the power structures at work within the Austrian asylum system is the critical exploitation of mapping as a research and design tool. Developed in three consecutive design courses on architecture and migration at the Institute of Architecture and Design at TU Wien, "Fluchtraum Österreich" not only produced spatial representations of the conditions found but also combined both physical and non-physical aspects into socio-spatial arguments, thereby creating both a catalogue of demands for the spatial standards of asylum accommodations in Austria and a much needed research basis for spatial practitioners wanting to become active participants within the asylum and hospitality fields. The catalogue of demands takes on the form of multi-dimensional visualizations that bring the invisible, the unknown, and the consciously hidden,[6] in this case the depoliticized refugees, into the architectural and public discourse.

The mapping examples shown here have been constructed in a constant feedback loop with the refugees in the Austrian federal states of Vienna, Styria, Carinthia, Tyrol, and Burgenland. This close collaboration not only puts the "invisible" refugees onto the (political) map but also goes beyond picturing refugees as simple cartographic subjects. Several workshops creating sociospatial mappings, exhibitions, and public discussions allowed the refugees to become active mapping agents within the political arena and opened up the opportunity for them to (re-)

gain their public voice. *An example of the collaborative methodology is Lea Soltau's mapping "Living Biography" (fig. 9), which continuously developed during a series of conversations with Mrs. H and her daughter. The visualization maps the spaces that the two women stayed in over the course of nine years, starting from their escape from Ramallah to multiple accommodations in Austria. While the level of detail increased to the description of tapestries, the daily routines, and the family's favorite places, it also became evident that they were still far from a condition of living, remaining instead in a state of being-located. The mapping shows that self-determination, retreat, and the possibility of creating personal atmosphere are basic needs of living; it also defines the spatial elements that could be implemented into the design of refugee hostels.*

Rather than being only a product, the mappings produced within the "Fluchtraum Österreich" research and teaching project are a catalyst for on-going debates and continue to be discussed in different forums, presentation, and exhibition formats.[7] The counter mappings are directed toward an audience that include refugees, providers of accommodation, NGOs, lawmakers, and architects; they can be read as a form of critique against the dominant power structures within the Austrian asylum system at various scales. At the same time, the visualizations become emancipatory tools for refugees by illustrating their desires and demanding their right to self-determination, privacy, inclusion, housing quality, employment, education, and political organization.

fig. 9 Lea Soltau — "Living Biography"

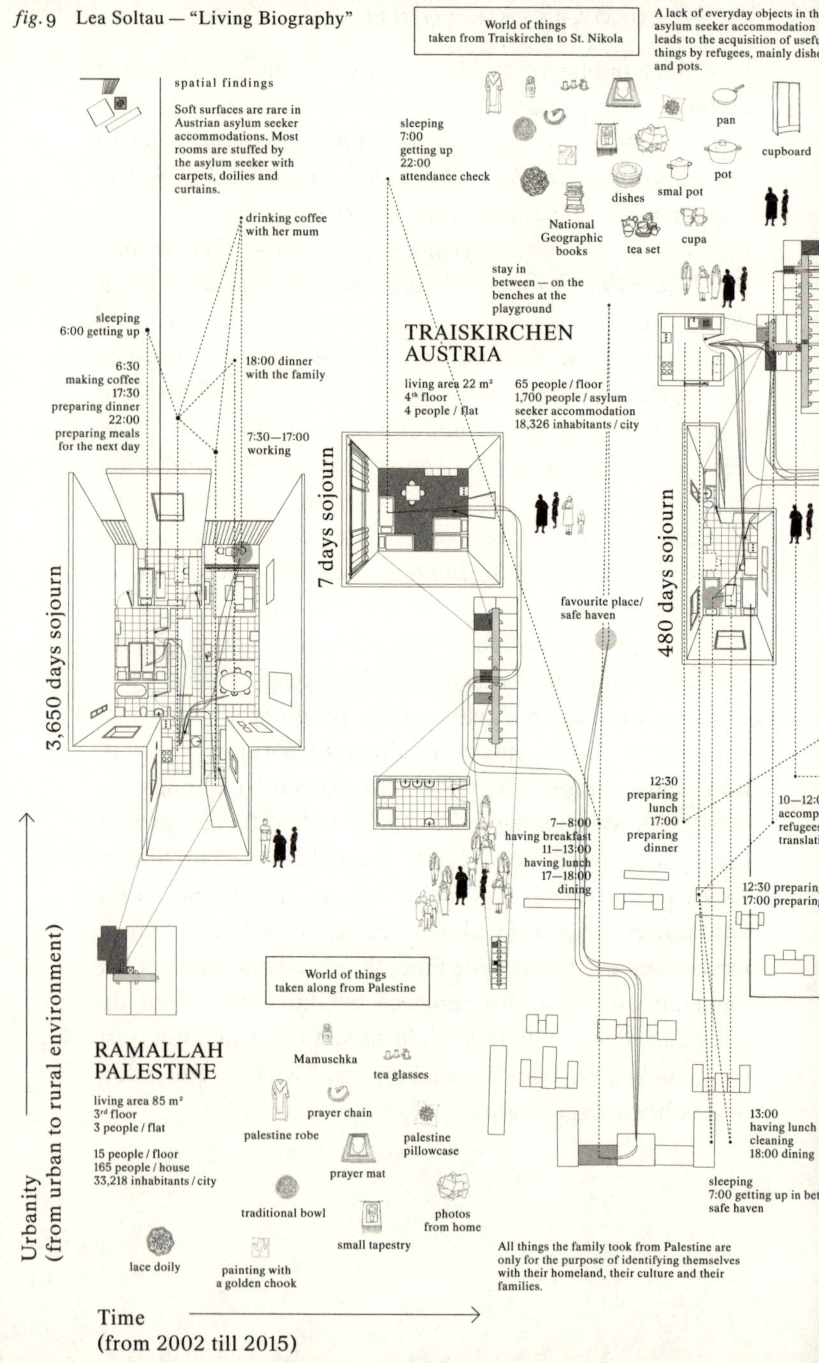

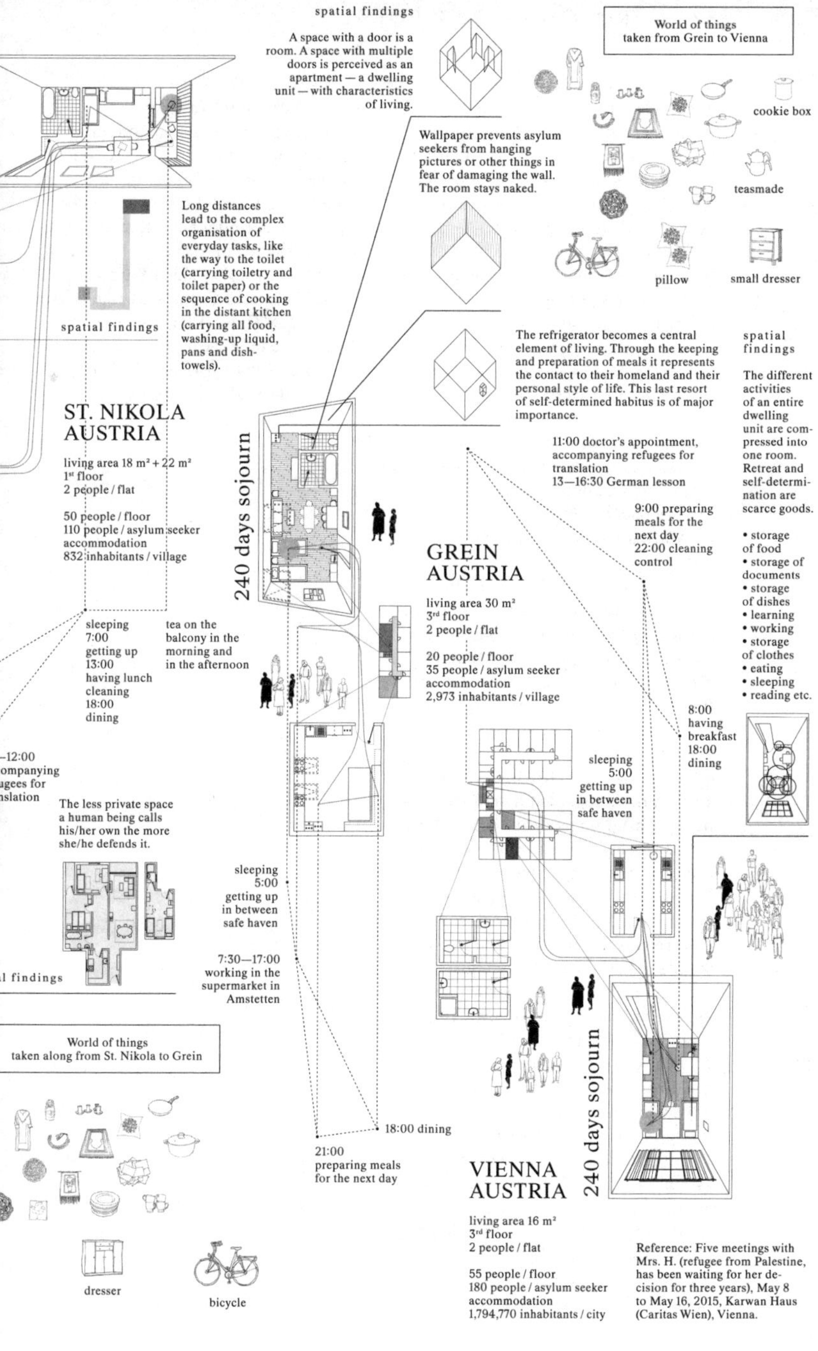
spatial findings
A space with a door is a room. A space with multiple doors is perceived as an apartment — a dwelling unit — with characteristics of living.
World of things taken from Grein to Vienna
cookie box
Wallpaper prevents asylum seekers from hanging pictures or other things in fear of damaging the wall. The room stays naked.
teasmade
Long distances lead to the complex organisation of everyday tasks, like the way to the toilet (carrying toiletry and toilet paper) or the sequence of cooking in the distant kitchen (carrying all food, washing-up liquid, pans and dish-towels).
pillow
small dresser
spatial findings
The refrigerator becomes a central element of living. Through the keeping and preparation of meals it represents the contact to their homeland and their personal style of life. This last resort of self-determined habitus is of major importance.
spatial findings
The different activities of an entire dwelling unit are compressed into one room. Retreat and self-determination are scarce goods.
ST. NIKOLA AUSTRIA
living area 18 m² + 22 m²
1st floor
2 people / flat
50 people / floor
110 people / asylum seeker accommodation
832 inhabitants / village
240 days sojourn
11:00 doctor's appointment, accompanying refugees for translation
13—16:30 German lesson
9:00 preparing meals for the next day
22:00 cleaning control
• storage of food
• storage of documents
• storage of dishes
• learning
• working
• storage of clothes
• eating
• sleeping
• reading etc.
GREIN AUSTRIA
living area 30 m²
3rd floor
2 people / flat
20 people / floor
35 people / asylum seeker accommodation
2,973 inhabitants / village
sleeping
7:00
getting up
13:00
having lunch
cleaning
18:00
dining
tea on the balcony in the morning and in the afternoon
8:00
having breakfast
18:00
dining
–12:00
:ompanying
ugees for
nslation
sleeping
5:00
getting up
in between
safe haven
The less private space a human being calls his/her own the more she/he defends it.
sleeping
5:00
getting up
in between
safe haven
7:30—17:00
working in the supermarket in Amstetten
l findings
World of things taken along from St. Nikola to Grein
18:00 dining
21:00
preparing meals for the next day
240 days sojourn
VIENNA AUSTRIA
living area 16 m²
3rd floor
2 people / flat
55 people / floor
180 people / asylum seeker accommodation
1,794,770 inhabitants / city
dresser
bicycle
Reference: Five meetings with Mrs. H. (refugee from Palestine, has been waiting for her decision for three years), May 8 to May 16, 2015, Karwan Haus (Caritas Wien), Vienna.

1 The German term "Unterbringung von Asylwerbern," in English "asylum seeker accommodation," represents the official term used by the Austrian authorities and is consciously used in this essay since the regulations that apply to this typology for housing refugees are at the center of our critique. Apart from that, we use the term "refugee" for a person that was forced to flee his or her home country, no matter in what stage of the Austrian asylum system he or she is currently in.

2 Fluchtraum Österreich is a long-term teaching and research project, focusing on spatial structures and boundaries constructed around asylum seekers in and outside Austria. → www.fluchtraum.at

3 Marina Gržinić, "A Refugee Protest Camp in Vienna and the European Union's Processes of Racialization, Seclusion, and Discrimination," *e-flux journal* 43 (March 2013). → https://www.e-flux.com/journal/43/60214/a-refugee-protest-camp-in-vienna-and-the-european-union-s-processes-of-racialization-seclusion-and-discrimination

4 This was especially important since Austria regained its independence in 1955, after being occupied by the Allied forces, and declared permanent political neutrality in its newly established constitution. See: Raimund Pehm, "Die Flüchtlingspension: Eine österreichische Besonderheit im Wandel," Lecture at the symposium "Ist Gast gleich Gast? Asylsuchende in österreichischen Tourismusarchitekturen," Architektur Haus Kärnten, Klagenfurt (April 7, 2016).

5 Vicki Täubig, *Totale Institution Asyl. Empirische Befunde zu alltäglichen Lebensführungen in der organisierten Desintegration* (Weinheim/München: Juventa Verlag, 2009).

6 Philippe Rekacewicz, ed., "Mapping Globalisation," *An Architektur: Produktion und Gebrauch gebauter Umwelt 13* (Berlin, May 2004); Denis Wood, *The Power of Maps* (New York: Guilford, 1992).

7 Asylum seeker accommodation in Gasthof Bärenwirt (2015), UNHCR Langer Tag der Flucht (2015), afo — architekturforum oberösterreich (2015), Akademie der bildenden Künste Wien (2015), Tonhof in Maria Saal, Kärnten (2015), Architektur Haus Kärnten (2016), Austrian Cultural Forum Berlin (2016), UN Habitat III Conference, Quito, Ecuador (2016), Venice Architecture Biennale (2016), and Universität der Künste Berlin (2017).

Pelin Tan

Architecture Pedagogy in Conflict Territories: Methods of Decolonization as an Immanence Criticism

The forms of critique are multiple. The usual intention in architectural critique is centered around form and function. Having been trained in social science that is very human and socius-centered, I find it challenging, to take the architectural form and the design element as the core of the empiric subject that provides unexpected layers of critique about *worlding*.[1] But what are the dimensions and scales of such critique? What are the related practices and their effects? How do the conditions and power matter in such practices? What is the role of an entangled ontology in the relations between such spatial entities? The questions can be expanded. Firstly, I believe that pedagogy in architecture could be a form of critique that not only influences students but also is the very institutional structure of an university. Pedagogy has its baggage of the history of criticism that is very much informed by the thoughts of thinkers and practitioners, such as Paulo Freire or Ivan Illich. The discussions and practices of alternative pedagogy, critical pedagogy, or decolonization pedagogies have greatly influenced the social science education in terms of criticism and methodology in research practices. The current neoliberalization, work-labor conditions, and the market's demand strongly affect the ways education is forming itself. Therefore, the field of not only architecture education but also education in general shows that the impact of neoliberalization and conservatism is huge in contemporary pedagogical structures forcing to reduce criticism as much as possible.[2] An outcome of the critique of the impact in many educational institutions, the pedagogical criticism and praising alternatives have been inherited from the discourses of the 1970s capitalist class struggle and, furthermore, the postcolonial discourses by thinkers like Gayatri Spivak or Edward Said at the end of the 1990s.

Territorialities/Exception/Arazi

State of exception is stated by sovereignty, as Carl Schmitt describes in his "Political Theology."[3] This argument is based on political and judicial power. For Giorgio Agamben, "the state of exception is not a special kind of law (like the law of war), rather, insofar as it is a suspension of the juridical order itself, it defines law's threshold or limit concept."[4] By analyzing Carl Schmitt's theory of the state of exception, Agamben inserts that "'being-outside' and 'belonging' is the 'topological structure of state of exception,' and only because the sovereign, who decides on the exception, is, in truth, logically defined in his being by the exception, [...]."[5] So in relation to space or topos, *exception* is a practice of hegemony of de-territorialization by territorializing: a form of practice of excluding by including. For Agamben, the original political relation is "the ban, the state of exception as zone of indistinction between outside and inside, exclusion and inclusion."[6] If we look at it from the perspective of spatial practices, it is a formation of space demarcation. For the last ten years, the discussions and interpretations of *exception* in terms of topography and urbanism have been extended with examples of the extra-territorialities of phenomena, such as civil wars, occupied territories, liquid borderlines, islands, buffer zones, curfew cities, state-led urban transformations, and evictions. The contemporary experience of *exception* as a form is a multiple constellation that exists in a tension between territorial facts, objects, and subjectivities.

How does *territory* speak to us? What is its methodology and its fiction? The term *Arazi*, used a lot in architectural and urban design studios to describe a *project space*, is an Ottoman word of Arabic origin that has many meanings, such as land, country, terrain, territory, estate, property, soil, ground, agricultural land, demanded land. Etymologically, the word is based on *Arz*, which means *supply* Its another origin could be *Araz*, which means *symptom*. In English, together with my research collective, I prefer to use *Arazi* as an equivalent of *territory*, which may not fully correspond to it because the direct translation of *territory* means *bölge* (region) or *territoryal* in Turkish. While this may not be the case in the social sciences, in architectural studios in Turkey Arazi is used as a term for space upon which the building has to be designed and constructed on. Arazi is also often understood as *tabula rasa,* — e.g. an empty plot in an urban environment or along the endless space in Anatolian cities, an abandoned land, a demolished land, a geological space with soil, stones, sometimes garbage without a trace of human action or history. It could be an innocent space or a ruin. I aim to bring back the understanding of the word both as a *territory* and as a concept relating to today's critical spatial research and practice. The effects of war and the negotiation of borderlines transform our approach and the methodologies of infrastructures. They are not only the functional thresholds of architecture but also the instrumentalization of new conditions that are part of *geontologies* of landscape. According to Elizabeth Povinelli, *geontologies* bring together two terms: *geos* (non-life) and *being* (ontology), which "are currently in play in the late liberal governance of difference and markets."[7] She proposes a new definition of biopolitics with no separation between elements of *life* and *non-life*, this combined conceptual approach is based on new figures, tactics, and discourses of power.[8] How can we approach the infrastructure of landscape shaped by war and migration from this theoretical perspective? What is the base to discuss such extra-territorialities through and with *Things*?

Infrastructure is a term for designing the modern urban space and for producing complete spatial objects. For centuries, it has held a basic role in colonization processes through introducing infrastructure projects in order to change and colonize cultures and societies in any scale. It also functions as a justification of neoliberal urban-rural policies in expanding, expropriating, and rescaling property and land. It is the object between form and law. As Easterling defines, "Infrastructure is considered to be a hidden substrate—the binding medium or current between objects of positive consequence, shape, and law."[9] Recently, the discourses of infrastructure have revealed the role of infrastructure in more complex ways. Incomplete and failing infrastructure often relate to the character of the infrastructural functions that prolong the process of infrastructure projects, which becomes more important than the complete infrastructure itself, with actors, such as the state, local governments, developers, and citizens, debate or negotiate, thereby leading to more profit and surplus. In short, instead of a complete object or a presentation, the incomplete, the continuous failure, or the process of infrastructure becomes a vital part. It is often argued that in many cases (in Indian cities, for example) the failure of infrastructure or the interruption of the infrastructural function brings about the co-existences of alternative infrastructure in the networks of such cities.

Infrastructure as an assemblage is another current discourse of infrastructure. As Stephen Graham describes, "urban infrastructures as complex assemblages that bring all manner of human, non-human, and natural agents into a multitude of continuous liaisons across geographic space."[10]

Around the city of Mardin, Turkey, close to the Syrian border, we have faced many official refugee camps, self-organized camps, and temporary dwellings of migrants as an outcome of the civil war in Syria since 2013. Together with my students, we have run several workshops and studios on the permanency and temporariness of tent dwellings and the life forms in temporary habitats. We have understood such dwellings as entangled infrastructures through which we can learn about self-design and architecture instead of teaching camp designing. I see urbanized and temporary refugee camp settlements as forms of *decay*, a subtractive building process that is about both an anachronism and a decay of architecture itself. I see the experience of such *ad hoc* infrastructure (camps or tents) not in the total context of a state of emergency or a limited spatial form of exception. The decay of forms compels us to deal with anachronisms that do not withhold the *in-humanity* rooted in human history.

When Reza Negarestani asks, "Is decay a positive or a negative building process?," he adds that "the building process of decay is subtractive, which is to say, it is concurrently intensively negative and extensively positive."[11] The contraction of the negative and positive sides of the process of decay, the subtraction of forms, comprises the potentials — the infinite latitudes of forms. Negarestani's first axiom is that "decay is a building process, it has a chemical slant and a differential [...] dynamic distribution. The process of decay builds new states of extensity, affect, magnitude, and even integrity from and out of system or formation without nullifying or reforming it."[12] I suggest that refugee camps as a spatial form are part of the process of building an infrastructure that deterritorializes the refugee as an arche-fossil of the posthuman era. The possible putrefaction of arche-fossils, together with the time involved in the formation processes, concerns the relation of anachronism to *decay*. "The process of decay generates differential forms by limitropically subtracting from the rotten object," writes Negarestani, defining the architecture and politics of decay that can be read through the constellations of objects and models.[13] Warfare, ecological disaster, and technological collapse deeply impact our everyday lives and designate our future spatial infrastructures. Ecological disasters are the core reasons for governments to issue policies for the further demolishment of ecological landscapes and inhabitants. In the case of refugee camps, sustaining livelihood, such as dwelling, food, health, and emergency related issues, are the basic forces behind zoning a camp plan. This form of dwelling and its zoning plan are a production of space, a continuous negotiation of public space, based on several facts, such as border politics and its juridical justifications, humanitarian aid negotiations, and political agencies. Camp design programs aim to supply the dwelling needs of a community in a spatial scale of a neighborhood, a village, or a small city.

Refugee communities are often taken as homogenous entities, with their kinship, tribal, and religious networks being dismissed.

Transversal Method

Transversal methodology in architectural education and research is necessary as both social and spatial scales are fluid according to the assemblages and entanglements of infrastructures and materials. Therefore, the methodology of a pedagogy grounded with a decolonial positioning is transversal from digital techniques to action research and engaged participation. Thinking transversally about architecture allows for trans-local and borderless knowledge production that rhizomatically extends beyond the familiar terrains of architecture and design, thereby encompassing issues such as citizenship, militant pedagogy, institutionalism, borders, war, being a refugee, documents and documenting, urban segregation, commons, and others. Félix Guattari describes transversality as an analytic method that cuts across multiple fields, often affiliated with models of knowledge and pedagogy such as *assemblage methods* or *affective pedagogy*: "[...] neither institutional therapy, nor institutional pedagogy, nor the struggle for social emancipation, but, which invoked an analytic method that could transverse these multiple fields (from which came the theme 'transversality'."[14]

Methodology is not only a system for describing realities, but also a political tool that takes part in knowledge production. "Method assemblage," as described by John Law, is the process of enacting or crafting bundles of ramifying relations that condense presence and (therefore also) generate absence by shaping, mediating, and separating the two.[15] Often, method assemblage is about manifesting realities out there and the depictions of such realities in-here. Law's work, which mainly concerns critical approaches of methods for social sciences, also reveals methodological openings, which I think have a potential for architectural research and pedagogies.

In the meanwhile, *affective pedagogy* refers to Deleuze's reference to Spinoza's concept of "affect/affections," i.e. a type of perception that moves beyond the body and assemblages of form:

> "Affect is a starting place from which we can develop methods that have an awareness of the politics of aesthetics: methods that respond with sensitivity to aesthetic influence on human emotions and understand how they change bodily capacities."[16]

The discursive potentialities of form, together with the question as to how the matter of form can be outside the control of the architect's mind, exceeds the post-structuralist critique of Cartesian dualism. These concepts allow thinking of new multiplicities for pedagogy and practice, thereby enabling a more transversal form of architecture. Such a materialist approach is also about the theoretical grounding and methodological challenge of analyzing, understanding, and situating an architectural form in its ontological foundation. Nick J. Fox and Pam Alldred describe the research assemblage in their new materialist approach of social inquiry that I think could support architectural design and methods. They explain a materialist approach in research:

> "It supplies a conception of agency not tied to human action, shifting the focus for social inquiry from an approach predicated upon humans and their bodies, examining instead how relational networks or assemblages of animate and inanimate affect and are affected."[17]

I think such an approach on the matter or thing in research can be very specific in territorial conditions. Such conditions and shifting liquid spaces affect the structures and conditions of architecture; therefore, not only the product or form of architecture as an outcome but also the dynamics of several conditions of architecture is produced in total ways.

I understand the notion of transversality as a practice in which both epistemic and theoretical categories are transversal, replacing each other. It is also a practice embedded bodily in everyday life. The "institution/instituting" element is a part of it. Thus, creating such a practice also influences the political body of an institution and the way we institute. When I consider myself teaching in architecture, in different productions and representations of knowledge as relating to small-scale design, larger than the knowledge in different levels of integrated disciplines (such as sociology, sciences, or art), I feel that it is a powerful tool that could be carried further with students. Students' actions are part of the togetherness in the transversality of pedagogy. The understanding of such methodology is often affiliated with terms in alternative knowledge and pedagogy practices that are often described as *assemblage methods* or *affective pedagogy*.

Teaching as a colonizer in a territory is a problematic position; therefore, assemblage methods are closely related to creating radicalism with the colonized subjectivity, in which my colonizer's identity would not be based on a fundamental justification of a politically correct emancipatory act, as well as an endlessly informed sense of guilt. The research projects and the education that I am involved in Southeast Anatolia, near the Syrian border in the Kurdish-Arabic zone, is an architecture faculty that was established by my colleagues some years ago. Designing an architectural education has two aims for me: 1) to abandon the style and types of pedagogy (in theory and design studios) that belong to a typical architecture faculty by investing new types of materialist methods, and 2) working on urgent socio-political issues that concern this geography, one that has officially been a war zone for many years. In this region, territorial cases demand new methodological tools and design studio structures, such as military architecture (water dams, security zones), forensic cases about extra-juridical murders, refugee camps, borders as liquid spaces, evicted villages, state-led ecology discourse as colonization, and urban transformation projects relating to land ownership and land-grabbing. The role of the 'architect,' the tools of architecture, and the knowledge of architecture need to tackle such territorial realities. Therefore, educational structures are based on the urgency of renewing transversal methods.

I established the Forensik Mimarlık research together with my graduate students, it came out of the discussions we had during our graduate seminars, inspired by the forensic methodological research in conflict zones. Forensik Mimarlık focuses on several actors, such as human right activists, mayors, and actors who lead the production of the spatial development of Mardin and its region. A traumatic zone after the intense civil war between the Turkish government and the Kurdish movement, the territory has been a space of judicial incidents to be analyzed. The Human Rights Association of Mardin, involved in the investigation of extra-judicial killings and the forensic bone identification process, has been excavating the land around the region. Forensik Mimarlık observes the process of how the territory, officially defined by hegemonic structures as *tabula rasa*, needs to be analyzed and decolonized by research and a new conceptualization based on concrete cases. The recently implemented border politics between Syria, Iraq, and Turkey has led many refugees to flee to the southeast region where a lot of refugee camps settlements expanded. Forensik Mimarlık involves students in research on camps and in direct communication as they are Kurds and Arab who speak the same languages. They are directly involved in instant architecture, emergency architecture, and related conceptual discussions. Forensik Mimarlık also researches the decolonization of the language of architecture in this region, exploring future design proposals for the currently fast-urbanizing territory. Affective pedagogy is a part of this research as it is based on an instant involvement with the region's actors, as well in the graduate theses, course actions of these topics and themes.

Decolonization Pedagogy

I consider the practice of *decolonization* both as epistemically extreme territorial conditions and as a modernist theoretical category in the architectural discipline. The basic principles for a decolonizing educational structure include: 1) constructing non-hegemonic knowledge through a collective process, and 2) creating an instituting practice without remaining or fully reaching out to an *institution*. Education is, by default, a fully instituting structure through which an institution itself becomes a machine for the sake of sustaining itself. What is a collective process in such education? It entails destroying the hierarchy of the dualist structures between a teacher and a student, as well as teaching and learning. Furthermore, it means collective self-teaching, learning by acting together, rejecting the gap between theory and practice, deconstructing terms in education sustained by institutions, and preserving traditional knowledge from earth and nature. The methodology, the syllabus, and the topic-based content are the base for a any

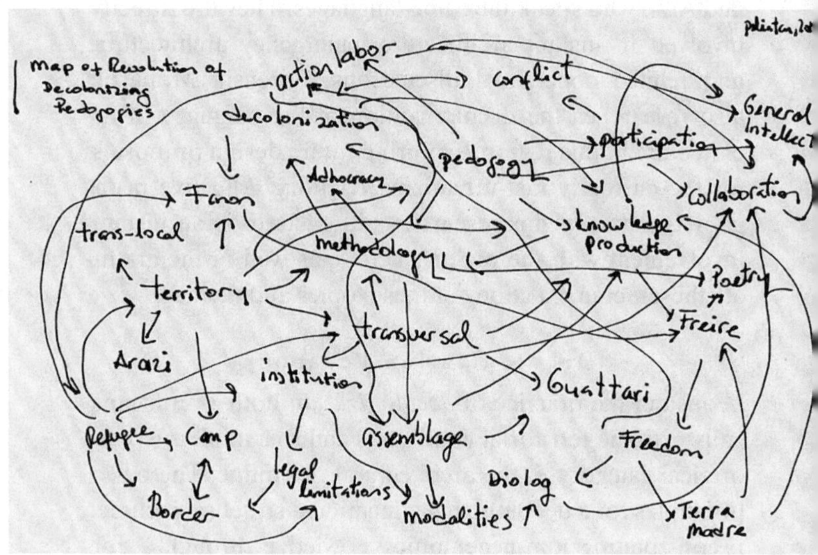

fig. 10 Decolonizing Pedagogies

pedagogy. Education in architecture is often trapped in between the architectural genres of specific territorial conditions and the global conflict of form-concept relations that conservatively inform the syllabus and design studio programs, which is why I feel that it always requires two processes to occur: 1) decolonizing the architectural knowledge from a certain hegemonic territorial condition that a specific form of institutionalization is attached to, and 2) creating transversal methodology that exceeds the form and concept in design.

In education, the term *decolonization* is often discussed within the 20th century legacy of Fanon and Freire. This increasingly important term signifies not only institutional criticism but also a search of alternative knowledge production in different colonizer-colonized structures. In the context of the colonizer-colonized dyad, *decolonization* concerns not only resisting against territorial occupation and violence but also transforming institutions, cultural products, approaches, and values. Moreover, in the context of pedagogy, *decolonization* signifies a non-institutional education where knowledge is produced and shared collectively. While university or academia is considered the main place for the production and dissemination of knowledge, alternative structures and ways of knowledge production, such as collective research and its representation via social media, are the main formation of non-institutional structures or 'becoming' institutions. Transversality is the practice through which knowledge is cross-created and disseminated. Such research processes and non-institutional structures can create a real effect, taking part in the social-political transformation both in the mainstream institutions and society. For example, in Southeast Anatolia, where our faculty is based, waterdams are expanding. As this context is one of the main concerns in our graduate education, we take the waterdam as a building typology and a spatial reality that is a colonizing strategy of the Turkish Government in order to dispose the land and create surveillance tools instead of concerning its ecological outcome.[18] Observing and analyzing this development, graduate students (architects and planners) are able to create a counter-knowledge of the role of a spatial development that can lead to acts of decolonization in the near future. Eve Tuck and K. Wayne Yang argue that "decolonization is a metaphor:" "The easy adoption of decolonizing discourse by educational advocacy and scholarship, evidenced by the increasing number of calls to 'decolonize our schools,' or use 'decolonizing methods,' or, 'decolonize student thinking,' turns decolonization into a metaphor."[19]

The critical stance they elaborate gives an in-depth insight into understanding why we use this term in pedagogy. They continue that "decolonization as metaphor allows people to equivocate these contradictory decolonial desires because it turns decolonization into an empty signifier to be filled by any track towards liberation."[20] For them, anti-colonial critique and decolonization are slightly different. I think that their critique helps to understand the term better. On the other hand, the dualistic structures of colonizers and oppressed subjectivities are nowadays more complex and vary from territory to territory (if we take Fanon's ideas as a base for dualistic structure of the colonizer and the colonized, similar in Freire's approach). In my opinion, using the word as a metaphor has the emancipative power to reconsider in our methodologies, process-based research tools, and complex realities of territories, as well as the actors in the social production of architecture. In "Decolonizing Knowledge," Alessandro Petti explains that the basic infrastructure in the first intifada in Palestine was not available, and reaching education was not possible for children and young people; therefore, self-sufficiency and collectively maintaining the commons became an important life condition for Palestinians in the occupied territories. Self-education and collective teaching became a tool of autonomy.

> "Theoretical knowledge was combined with one that emerges from action and experimentation. Learning became a crucial tool for gaining freedom and autonomy. People discovered that they could share knowledge and could be in charge of what and how to study [...]. The classical structure, in which 'expert teachers' transmit knowledge and students are mere recipients to be filled with information, was substituted by a blurred distinction between the two."[21]

Alessandro Petti adds that such an education practice has become a tool of empowerment and emancipation, which is vital for Palestinians for decolonization in the occupied territories.

Another pedagogical example is the case of Cyprus as a divided island, a territorial land of colonial exploitation. The island has been occupied by the military infrastructures of Great Britain, the UN, Greece, and, since 1974, Turkey. The urban design studio (Fall 2018, 3rd year) aimed to speculate the future withdrawal of military bases, abandoning the infrastructure. With the students, we propose several scenarios how the military infrastructures could be decolonized and its architectural elements could be transformed into spaces of the commons. Architect and educator Socrates Stratis (AA+U, Nicosia) has been working for the past 15 years in Cyprus on decolonial pedagogical tools and future design speculations for the possibilities to converge two segregated communities (Greek and Turkish), facing the constraints of the territory, as well as the colonial mentalities inert in the society. Referring to his past studio experiences and its pedagogical approach, Stratis explains:

> "Critical pedagogy has become a valid approach to open up the architectural education to reconciliation processes focusing on the urban environment where peace-building takes place. Reconciliation departs from a negative peace building process where each community in conflict, in our case the Greek Cypriot as well as the Turkish Cypriot, challenges its dominant narratives about the 'other.'"[22]

This pedagogical radicality concerns asking further questions about knowledge production in architectural education. Upon what local conditions and extraterritorial constraints and in what traditions of the architectural history does it happen? The radical questioning of the architectural discipline is deeply rooted in architectural education that still resists going beyond studio work, mainstream design methodologies, crossing multiple disciplines, and considering trans-local territories. We are urged to alter our research methods through trans-disciplinary thinking based on borrowing cross-methods, new media that would provide performative visual representation tools, and engagement as militant researchers in everyday life in order to experience other knowledges or the multiplicity of knowledge production. Reformulating forms of reactions in syllabi, design studios, and politics of academic structures of architecture faculties will lead to inventing new pedagogies.

Conclusion

I claim that the pedagogical tools and processes in architectural education can function as decolonial emancipative processes and criticism on the entangled power structure.

Such criticism not only points to the popular neoliberal criticism, the spatial organization of oppression, and the means of outlaw territories,[23] but also aims to reveal the architecture of insurgency, counter-spatialities of resistance, and solidarity. Furthermore, radical pedagogy includes a decolonial process as collective thinking and proceeding into action. The formation of criticism includes challenging and transforming the theoretical concepts such as territory, biopolitics, colonialism, landscape, infrastructure, material, exception, and pedagogy strongly rooted in the Western-oriented epistemology by re-claiming through research and pedagogical practices in outlaw territories. This reclamation of "otherwise" should decolonize the criticism of the 20th century Western-Europe-oriented conceptual framework so that pedagogy and radical research in architecture and design can be its vital part.

1 "The notion of 'worlding' arising from non-representational theory provides a useful lens through which process of human-non-human enmeshment can be considered." → http://newmaterialism.eu/almanac/w/worlding (accessed 20 April 2019).

2 State and private universities, as well as the education systems in various countries, differ in terms of the means of democratization, still, there is a strong global tendency toward neoliberalization and conservatism in education.

3 "Sovereign is he who decides on exception." Carl Schmitt, *Political Theology: Four Chapters of Sovereignty*, trans. George Schwab (Chicago: The University of Chicago Press, 2005), 5.

4 Giorgio Agamben, *State of Exception*, trans. Kevin Attell (Chicago: The University of Chicago Press, 2005), 4.

5 Ibid., 35.

6 Ibid.

7 Elisabeth A. Povinelli, *Geontologies — A Requiem To Late Liberalism* (Durham and London: Duke University Press, 2016), 5.

8 Ibid.

9 Keller Easterling, *Extrastatecraft*, (New York: Verso, 2016), 17.

10 Stephen Graham, ed., *Disrupted Cities: When Infrastructure Fails* (London: Routledge, 2010), 1—26.

11 Reza Negasterani, "Undercover Softness: An Introduction to the Architecture and Politics of Decay," *COLLAPSE VI: Geo/Philosophy* (2010), 382.

12 Negarestani, "Undercover," 382

13 Ibid.

14 Pierre-Félix Guattari, "Institutional Practice and Politics. An Interview by Jacques Pain," in *The Guattari Reader*, ed. Gary Genosko (Oxford: Blackwell Publisher, 1996), 121.

15 John Law, *After Method: Mess in the Social Science Research,* London and New York: Routledge 2004, 122.

16 Anna Hickey-Moody, "Aesthetics and affective pedagogy," in *Deleuze and Research Methodologies*, eds. Rebecca Coleman and Jessica Ringrose (Edinburgh: Edinburgh University Press, 2013), 79—95.

17 Nick J. Fox and Pam Alldred, "New Materialist Social Inquiry: Designs, Methods and the Research-Assemblage," *International Journal of Social Research Methodology* 18, no. 4 (2015): 399—414.

18 Zeynep S. Akinci and Pelin Tan, "Waterdams as Dispossession: Ecology, Security, Colonization," in *Climates: Architecture and the Planetary Imaginary*, eds. James Graham, Caitlin Blanchfield, Alissa Anderson, Jordan Carver, and Jacob Moore (Zurich: Lars Müller Publisher, 2016), 142—148.

19 Eve Tuck and K. Wayne Yang, "Decolonization Is Not a Metaphor," *Decolonization: Indigeneity, Education & Society* 1, no. 1 (2012): 1—40.

20 Tuck and Yang, 7.

21 Alessandro Petti, "Decolonizing Knowledge" (2014), available at: → www.campusincamps.ps/democratizing-knowledge-production/ (accessed 20 April 2019).

22 Socrates Stratis, ed., *Guide to Common Urban Imaginaries in Contested Spaces* (Berlin: Jovis Verlag, 2016), 241.

23 Felicity D. Scott, *Outlaw Territories — Environments of Insecurity/Architectures of Counterinsurgency* (Massachussettes: MIT Press, 2016).

Matteo Trentini

The Inevitability of Crisis: Manfredo Tafuri between Venice and Red Vienna

Der Bürger deiner wandernden Stadt,
Er weiß, diese Stadt ist sein Alles [1]
FRANZ GRILLPARZER, Feldmarschall Radetzky

History serves to dispel nostalgia,
not to inspire it.[2]
MANFREDO TAFURI

This essay investigates the significance of the early 20th century Viennese intellectual production on the historiographic project of architectural historian Manfredo Tafuri and, in more general terms, on the Institute of History of Architecture at the Istituto Universitario di Architettura di Venezia (IUAV) in the 1970s.[3] Tafuri's critical approach to the architectural production of Red Vienna must be read in the context of how the figure of *Krisis*[4] in the early 20th-century Viennese thought was reflected within the Institute. The Venetian Institute was interested in creating what Patrizia Lombardo defines as a more general "theory of the metropolis"[5] as an expression of the intellectual ten-

fig. 11 Manfredo Tafuri, Vienna Rossa, 1981

sion — coined by Tafuri, who paraphrases Simmel as *das Nervenleben*[6] — of and within a large city.[7] This essay aims to reconstruct the role that Vienna's "Merry Apocalypse"[8] had on the plan to write a Marxist theory of the metropolis.

During the 1977—78 academic year, Manfredo Tafuri held a monographic course named "*La grande Vienna. Dalla formazione del mito asburgico alla crisi dell'Austromarxismo*" ("The great Vienna: From the Habsburg Myth to the Crisis of Austromarxism.") at the IUAV. This was one of the few courses (later on followed by his courses on Venice and Rome during the Renaissance) that Tafuri devoted entirely to a single city.[9] The seminar was the culminating point of a broader intellectual reflection on Vienna and its early 20th century cultural production, to which Tafuri returned several times. Already in 1971, he published an essay "Austromarxismo e città: Das Rote Wien"[10] ("Austromarxism and the city: Red Vienna") in the Italian Marxist magazine *Contropiano*, where he explored Vienna's residential politics under the socialist administration in 1919—1933.[11]

Tafuri's lectures not only were part of the broader and ongoing scientific research on the architectural production in Vienna in the early 20th century, but also offered, if read within a wider intellectual constellation, the opportunity to develop a constant intellectual and critical reference for the Venetian department in the person of Tafuri, its head since 1968, and the group of his collaborators there.

While in the late 1970s, the research into the Austrian culture found in the IUAV, a renowned centre of intellectual speculation, that large sections of the Italian culture had already shown a renewed and ongoing interest in the 20th century Middle European and Viennese culture. In 1957, the publishing house Einaudi printed the first Italian edition of Robert Musil's *The Man without Qualities* and, in 1964, Ludwig Wittgenstein's *Tractatus Logicus-Philosophicus*. In parallel, the early 20th century architectural production in Vienna was the centre of a wide historiographic analysis, which focused mainly on the "difficult" figure of Adolf Loos, as was the case of the monograph *Casabella-continuità* (1959, with a contribution from, among others, young Aldo Rossi), dedicated to the author of the house on Michaelerplatz.[12] In 1963, literary historian Claudio Magris published with Einaudi his *Il mito asburgico nella letteratura austriaca moderna* ("The Habsburg Myth in Austrian Modern Literature"),[13] which inspired Tafuri's choice of the title of his 1977—78 Venetian course. The book historically reconstructed the significance of the Habsburg myth[14] of a civilization "that, in the name of its love for order, discovers the disorder of the world."[15] This tragic aspect of the modern Middle-European *Kultur* as an anticipation of the inevitable *Krisis*[16] can also be found in his 1971 essay in *Contropiano* on the architectural production in Red Vienna. At that time, the magazine was one of the leading intellectual platforms for the Italian Marxist left-wing, with its cultural project of a "critique of ideology" as an opportunity to verify "the tasks that the capitalistic development took away from architecture."[17]

Tafuri's essays cannot be separated from the critical project of *Contropiano*, which, in the field of architecture, aimed at a "coherent Marxist criticism against the architectural and urban ideology that can do nothing but demystify the incidental and historical realities — not at all objective nor universal — that lie behind the unifying categories of the terms art, architecture, city."[18] In the light of the political debate that started within *Contropiano*, Red Vienna became the first case of a city being addressed by a critique of ideology. Indeed, while all the topics studied in the journal (Weimar Germany, post-revolutionary Russia, or the attempts of the American city planning of the New-Deal) were analyzed as larger political and territorial entities, the analysis of the Viennese situation referred to the specific scale of an individual city. This peculiarity, as we will see later in this essay, significantly influenced Tafuri's analysis of the housing policy of the Social Democratic Workers' Party (SDAPDÖ). The detailed reflection on the Viennese case, however, had for him also a precise historiographic relevance. As Tafuri states at the beginning of his investigation,[19] the essay filled the historiographic silence over the Viennese experience, the silence perpetuated by Bruno Zevi (1950)[20] and Leonardo Benevolo (1960),[21] the two main text books of the history of modern architecture, used at that time in Italy.[22]

For Tafuri and the *Contropiano* group, the focus on Vienna was a chance to concretize the necessity of expanding the critique of ideology to *all* neo-capitalist ideologies, including the reformist and social-democratic ones. This need was resumed in 1966, directly from the "merciless criticism of everything existing," which Marx had already spoken about by the philosopher Mario Tronti in his "Operai e Capitale,"[23] a future collaborator of *Contropiano.* Therefore, Tafuri's approach to Vienna as an "exceptional urban experience" for the total identification between technical and architectural expertise and political planning should be seen precisely within this need for the merciless criticism of everything existing. Faithful to the Marxist project of *Contropiano*, Tafuri reads Red Vienna as a social-democratic island within a country ruled exclusively by conservative forces, with the public housing program being the only occasion through which the party's political agenda would be made visible. It also allowed to assess the willingness of the architectural culture to embrace a *plan* which, on a local scale, would find an immediate translation into a concrete political action. After the first analysis of the theoretical and ideological foundations of this internal debate within the Austrian left-wing, which recognized, in Otto Bauer's program (1919),[24] the centrality of the housing issue, Tafuri immediately understood the contradiction and limitation of the political program being unable to push toward a crisis in the previous superstructural organization of a city, which was by then an "abnormal capital that during the 19th century had only outwardly taken the features of a modern *Grossstadt*, while it actually consolidated its facies of symbol-city of the imperial myth."[25]

By choosing to concentrate its political action mostly on the "housing issue," through which "demonstration models of fulfilled social democracy" would be organized,[26] the Viennese Social Democratic Workers' Party decided to leave behind the urban issue in its complexity, relegating it to the "negative legacy" of the city of the 19th-century speculative capitalism. In fact, as stated by Tafuri, although on a purely political level the action around the housing issue was fully legitimized — the 1917 census indicated that 73.1% of the housing stock consisted of sub-standard apartments — the Viennese social-democratic program appeared to be ineffective, if not totally absent, on the scale of urban planning.

The "fortresses" constituted by the Viennese blocks, being a "gigantic display of the new proletarian ethics,"[27] we are made not to subvert but to criticize the city of the aggressively speculative capitalism of the 19th century, with disastrous working-class housing conditions being among its drastic and most immediate effects. According to Tafuri, the limited efficacy of the Viennese program on the urban scale was an ideological problem: the political isolation of Red Vienna within the entirely conservative nation played a crucial role in determining even the most strictly *formal* results of the Socialist administration's building production. For the local Social Democratic Workers' Party, the housing program was the only tangible opportunity to put into practice and finally make visible its political agenda to its supporters and, above all, its rivals. Each of the completed projects of Red Vienna's housing program was thus inevitably overcharged with a symbolic force, as it was asked to criticize and comment on the capitalist city's forms. Therefore, Red Vienna became the showcase city of a new socialist ethic that found in residential architecture its most immediately visible effects, "a sort of giant exhibition of the new proletarian ethics entrenched in the workers accommodation,"[28] in which there was neither space nor a programmatic ability to go beyond the formal criticism of the city of the 19th-century speculation. Tafuri's main criticism against the program of Viennese social democracy lies precisely in this inability and impossibility of the Social Democratic Worker's Party to articulate a real *counter-plan* ("contropiano") at the urban scale able to *radically*—literally from scratch—put in a crisis the structures and shapes of the previous city model, produced by capitalist speculation. At the moment that the urban battle between the social democratic and capitalist models within the capitalist state cannot even start, the political program of the Social Democratic Workers' Party is reduced to the rhetoric of the architectural language. According to Tafuri, the Viennese experience considered the city of the 19th-century speculation only a mere "unavoidable persistence to challenge."[29] It was not by chance, Tafuri continues, that Red Vienna's housing complexes for workers were located in the same urban plots that the

Christian Democrats' previous administration had already placed under the municipal control.[30] This not only involved an inevitable fragmentation between the various interventions beyond their typological differentiation, but also denied the possibility of an overall urban development plan for the new socialist city. According to Tafuri, the controversy about the processes and different types of intervention, which, during the building program's early years, opposed the open and flexible model of the German *Siedlung* in favor of the Viennese fully-equipped block, disappeared due to the lack of an overall plan that distinguished the Viennese experience.

Emblematic for the constructions of the program's first period was the case of Winarsky-Hof (1924—26) and its main architect Peter Behrens, a professor at the local art academy since 1922, assisted by renowned Viennese architects, such as Josef Hoffmann, Josef Frank, and Margarete Schütte-Lihotzky. To Tafuri, Winarsky-Hof, which was at that time one of the largest projects with its 534 accommodations, seemed to be influenced by the controversy over the type of intervention that accompanied the Viennese program's first period. It was divided into two distinct parts: a closed triangular block and a wider, more articulated central complex, which consisted of the western body, with the typical layout of the soon-to-prevail super-block model, and the main body, articulated and open toward the city through four major portals, influenced by the open model of *Siedlung*. Despite this oscillation between two typological models, the size, the public impact, and the services, or what Tafuri called the "ostentatious syntheticism" of the intervention, seemed to be the completion of a "coherent architectural ideology,"[31] which would serve as a template for the subsequent interventions of the *Plan*. The project, however, not only symbolized the impossibility of an unambiguous proposal of urban intervention, expressed by the contrast between the closing of the lower block and the relative permeability of the main complex, but it also could be read as a possible answer to "idle populism" and to the formalism that characterized previous complexes, as was the case of Hanusch-Hof, built in the same year by Clemens Holzmeister. Later on, Karl Ehn's work, defined by Tafuri as "undoubtedly the most significant among the interpreters of proletarian ethics as a recovery of architectural ideology,"[32] followed the line traced by Behrens and his two interventions carried out in 1924—1926. Ehn was the author of Karl-Marx-Hof, the "most complete synthesis between avant-garde contribution, structural emphasis and epic values emphasized by traditional styles."[33] The huge complex — 1,382 apartments distributed along five courtyards — combined the eclectic avant-garde realism with the bourgeois culture through an allusive assembly of forms. In Tafuri's opinion, the apparently secondary decorative elements, such as the flagpoles, established the definitive and absolute autonomy of the socialist urban fragment in contemporary Vienna. Its total autonomy — linguistic, functional, urban — made Karl-Marx-Hof a possible monument contrasting the negativity of the bourgeois city, with which no comparison but only radical non-involvement was possible, the gesture expressed through the deliberately introvert language of the superblocks.

It was perhaps no coincidence that after the realization of this "demonstrative monument,"[34] the Viennese administration's program started losing its ideological charge and, as Tafuri claims, the attention of the Viennese architectural culture moved toward aspects such as technological progress, prefabrication, and building site organization, which, by that time, the Viennese Social Democracy had left behind unlike its German counterpart. The symbolic power of projects such as Karl-Marx-Hof or George-Washington-Hof was abandoned around the 1930s, when incidentally the reactionary forces started attacks against the "red fortress." The architects of Red Vienna's program partially abandoned the previous linguistic rhetoric in favor of a stylistically more neutral logic of prefabrication to replace the worker's epos. This was the case of Rudolf Perco's complex of 1467 apartments on Friedrich-Engels-Platz. Here the "socialist realism" was no longer given by the "epic values" of Karl-Marx-Hof but rather by a general "poetry of discretion," expressed in the silent rhetoric of work and production. The drawings, provided by Perco to the municipal offices, document the in-depth analysis of the details, services, and construction techniques, marking the prevalence of what Tafuri calls "acceptance of the capitalist logic celebrated under the workers sign."[35] The architects' discourse no longer referred to the avant-garde of Karl-Marx-Hof or the "red fortresses" built along the Gürtel, but, as was the case of Weimar Germany, to the rationality of production and technological progress. The ideological and symbolic ethos of the first years of the program was then replaced. Once the architects realized their inability to affect the surrounding metropolitan reality, they were left with the "regressive utopia" of the shelter of technique and production, as well as the depletion of their own language. It is no coincidence that this development concurred with the masses' gradual loss of faith in the Party and the intensification of the fascist squads' attacks against the Red Vienna blocks, culminating in the assault on Karl-Marx-Hof in February 1934.[36]

In Red Vienna, which was the only case (apart from post-revolutionary Russia) where architecture became fully committed to a precise political agenda, the tool of the *Plan*, here in its urban extension, showed its inability to subvert and overcome the pre-existing order of the speculative city. For a culture as that of the early 20th century modern architecture, which had its own myth in the hope of the *Plan*, this was a clear signal of its own tragic crisis. In this sense, Tafuri sees Vienna as an emblem of the absence and fallibility of the *Plan*, understood as a tool with which to reform the city.

When speaking about Vienna, Tafuri employs the metaphor of an island, a red island surrounded by a "sea" of conservatism. He reads Vienna in the same way as another 20th century capital Manhattan, an island where Tafuri imagines Musil's Ulrich and his sister Agathe wrecking once they abandoned Cacania, looking for "the loneliness and the full immobility of continuous events of pure crystal"[37] of the "Millennial Kingdom." Therefore, Vienna is the city from where begins what Franco Rella — later Professor of Aesthetics at the same institute in Venice — calls "the historical space of the twentieth-century crisis."[38] In this sense, the specific perspective, through which Tafuri and his colleagues in Venice analyzed the case of Vienna, can be traced back to a broader reflection on the crisis of the modern *Kultur*, and therefore that of architecture and its language, around which the interest of the Department for Architectural history at the IUAV rotated.

In 1980, Tafuri writes that the "proletarian *Höfe* are indeed called to offer a synthesis. But doesn't the tradition of the great Viennese *Krisis* — which discovered that each language lives alone and that only in such solitude it may feel (and make feel) the presence of the other (*Das Andere*) — stand out in front of such a task?"[39] The crisis occurring in Vienna in the early decades of the 20th century was thus not limited to architecture but involved all of the different practices of intellectual and cultural work. In 1980, when analyzing the "solitude of the language" of Aldo Rossi—whose work he defines as composed of "emptied signs, planned exclusions, strict limitations"[40] —Tafuri resorts to Karl Kraus, Viennese *Sprachkritiker*, the critic of language *par excellence*, and his "In dieser großen Zeit" ("In These Great Times"), written in 1914, at the outset of the World War I tragedy:

> "Those who now have nothing to say, since the fact has the word, keep talking. Those who have something to say, come forward and be silent."[41]

Faced with the depletion of the word, Aldo Rossi's architecture could only become a distressed and silent comment to the tragic dissolution of the discipline. While the Krausian silence of Aldo Rossi's architectural work validated Tafuri's diagnosis on the crisis of modern architecture, the interest in Vienna's "Merry Apocalypse" continued, starting from the work by Rella, who, in his *Il silenzio e la parola* (1981), interprets negative thought as the "building of a critical knowledge,"[42] whose great legacy is, as Rella writes explicitly referencing Freud, "the analysis of the uneasiness—*das Unbehagen*—in civilization and in the subject divided within it."[43] Negative thought in its historical terms had already been Cacciari's focus in *Contropiano*[44] and in his essay collection "Pensiero negativo e razionalizzazione"[45] (1977). Cacciari's Viennese research converges in "Dallo Steinhof. Prospettive viennesi del primo Novecento,"[46] which starts from the Limoniberg, where Otto Wagner's church, as Cacciari writes, becomes the crossroads of the endless pilgrimages of those "posthumous men" who crossed the end of each subject.[47] That crossed the end of words.

Architecture, philosophy of negative thought, and the culture of *Krisis* found a fertile field to re-process in the particular cultural climate of the Institute for Architectural History at the IUAV in the 1970s. Here, "architecture as *built* word" uses literature in the same way as "literature as *spoken* word," which allows to speak about how *Krisis* uses architecture. It is not by chance that, as Cacciari states, one can follow "the endless pilgrimages and the endless follies that loom in this landscape" only from the Steinhof hill. This "might have started from the utopia that we left behind."[48]

The 20th century Vienna was a background to "endless pilgrimages" and "endless follies." It was also a city that itself felt that "alle Sätze sind gleichwertig"[49]: all sentences have the same value and may therefore be omitted. This is precisely what happens to the Looshaus on Michaelerplatz or to Lord Chandos by Hofmannsthal, another Viennese author frequently quoted by Tafuri, who was forced to discover with dismay that words "are vortexes that, looking at them, I sink with a sense of dizziness, they swirl without stopping, and after them one reaches the void."[50]

The radicality of Vienna's Merry Apocalypse resides exactly in the forced discovery of how one's words are *gleichwertig*, i.e. inevitably lacking in meaning. Against this folly of the modern metropolis, there is no possible *counterplan*, only the disenchantment of a "surrender without conditions."[51]

1 English translation: "Thy moving city's citizen,/ This city to him is all," → https://www.poetrynook.com/poem/field-marshal-radetzky
2 Manfredo Tafuri and Richard Ingersoll, "There is no Criticism, only History," *Common Place*, http://complace.j2parman.com/?p=263 (accessed October 3, 2018).
3 Tafuri displays specific interest in the architecture of Vienna at least three times: in his 1971 essay, in a monographic course (1977—78), and in a monographic book (1980). This specific analysis of the Viennese case — as is the theory supported in this essay — not only allowed to fill a partial void, at least in the Italian context, around certain facts about the early 20th century Viennese architecture but, thanks to the contemporary work within the Institute by such as Massimo Cacciari and Franco Rella, it also provided a crucial theoretical and critical reference for the historiographic activity of the Venice Institute.
4 Tafuri uses the term *Krisis* when he writes about "the tradition of the big Viennese Krisis" representing — in many fields (arts, literature, architecture, music) — the overcome of the old dialectic system in the late 19th- and early 20th century. See Manfredo Tafuri, *Vienna rossa. La politica residenziale nella Vienna socialista* (Milano: Electa, 1980), 42.
5 Patrizia Lombardo,"The Philosophy of the City," in Massimo Cacciari, *Architecture and Nihilism: On the Philosophy of Modern Architecture* (New Heaven — London: Yale University Press, 1993), xxxiv.
6 Manfredo Tafuri, *Progetto e utopia. Architettura e sviluppo capitalistico* (Roma — Bari: Laterza, 1973), 82.
7 Lombardo, xxxvii
8 see: Hermann Broch, *Hoffmansthal und seine Zeit. Eine Studie*. (München, Piper, 1964). Broch describes the intellectual climate in Vienna in the late 19th century with its social, intellectual and political rumblings leading to the collapse of the monarchy and later on, the arise of Nazism.
9 For an overview on the university lectures held by Tafuri in Venice, see: Andrew Leach, *Manfredo Tafuri. Choosing History* (Gent: A&S Books, 2007), 311 et seq.
10 Manfredo Tafuri, "Austromarxismo e città: 'Das Rote Wien,'" *Contropiano* 2, 1971.
11 The article would eventually become the final part of his monographic course of 1977—78 in Venice. Tafuri revised the course in 1980, changing its title to "Vienna Rossa. La politica residenziale nella Vienna socialista" ("The Red Vienna. Housing policy in Socialist Vienna"), and combined it with the collective catalogue that he curated for an exhibition at the Palazzo delle Esposizioni in Rome. Manfredo Tafuri, *Vienna rossa. La politica residenziale nella Vienna socialista* (Milano: Electa, 1980).
12 *Casabella-Continuità* 233, (1959).
13 Claudio Magris, *Il mito asburgico nella letteratura austriaca moderna* (Torino: Einaudi, 1963).
14 It was a constant reference and a mythological idea about the Era of the Habsburg Empire as found, for instance, in Joseph Roth's nostalgia or Robert Musil's *Kakania*.
15 Magris, Il mito asburgico, 4.
16 The term "Krisis" was used in its original ancient Greek version both from Tafuri and Caccari. See M. Tafuri, Vienna rossa, 42, and M. Cacciari, *Krisis. Saggio sulla crisi del pensiero negativo da Nietzsche a Wittgenstein* (Milano: Feltrinelli, 1976).
17 Manfredo Tafuri, *Progetto e utopia* (Roma — Bari: Laterza, 1973), 3.
18 Manfredo Tafuri, "Per una critica dell'ideologia architettonica," *Contropiano* (1969), 78.
19 Tafuri, "Austromarxismo e città," 259.
20 Bruno Zevi, *Storia dell'architettura moderna dalle origini al 1950*, (Torino: Einaudi, 1950)

21 Leonardo Benevolo, Storia dell'architettura moderna, (Roma—Bari: Laterza, 1960).
22 While Zevi makes no reference to the building program of socialist Vienna, Benevolo includes a photo of Karl Marx Hof, thereby underlining only the urbanist compactness of the Viennese blocks as a model opposing the shapes of the bourgeois city. See Benevolo, *Storia dell'architettura*, 550.
23 Mario Tronti, *Operai e capitale*, (Roma: Derive Approdi, 2006), 30 (first edition: M. Tronti, *Operai e capitale*, (Torino: Einaudi, 1966).
24 Otto Bauer, *Der Weg zum Sozialismus* (Vienna, 1919), qtd. in Tafuri, *Austromarxismo e città*, 266.
25 Tafuri, "Austromarxismo e città," 265.
26 Ibid., 273.
27 Ibid., 278.
28 Ibid.
29 Ibid.
30 Ibid., 290.
31 Ibid., 302.
32 Ibid., 304.
33 Ibid., 305.
34 Ibid., 306.
35 Translation by Lynda Scott, ibid., 310.
36 The "Februaraufstand" of February 1934 at Karl-Marx-Hof can been seen as the culmination of the civil war between the members of the Social Democratic Party and the Heimwehr troops.
37 Manfredo Tafuri, *La sfera e il labirinto. Avanguardie e architettura da Piranesi agli anni 70* (Torino: Einaudi, 1980), 215.
38 Franco Rella, *Il silenzio e le parole. Il pensiero nel tempo della crisi* (Milano: Feltrinelli, 1981), 138.
39 Tafuri, *Vienna rossa*, 42.
40 Tafuri, *La sfera*, 331.
41 Karl Kraus, "In dieser großen Zeit" in *Ausgewählte Werke in drei Bänden* (Berlin: Verlag Volk und Welt, 1971).
42 Ibid., 114.
43 Ibid., 58.
44 Massimo Cacciari, "Sulla genesi del pensiero negativo," *Contropiano* 1 (1969).
45 Massimo Cacciari, *Pensiero negativo e razionalizzazione* (Venezia: Marsilio editore, 1977). (Negative Thought and Rationalization)
46 Massimo Cacciari, *Dallo Steinhof. Prospettive viennesi del primo Novecento* (Milano: Adelphi, 1980). (From Steinhof. Viennese perspectives of the early twentieth century.)
47 Ibid., 17.
48 Ibid., 15.
49 Ludwig Wittgenstein, "Tractatus Logico-Philosophicus," in *Annalen der Naturphilosophie* (Leipzig: Unesma, 1921), 6.4 .
50 "Wirbel sind die, in die hinabzusehen mich schwindelt, die sich unaufhaltsam drehen und durch die hindurch mans ins Leere kommt." Hugo von Hofmannsthal, "Ein Brief " in *Gesammelte Werke in Einzelausgaben*, (Frankfurt: 1951), Italian edition curated by Claudio Magris, *Lettera di Lord Chandos* (Milano: Rizzoli, 1995), 45.
51 Manfredo Tafuri, "Lavoro intellettuale e sviluppo capitalistico," *Contropiano* 2 (1970), 254.

fig. 12 Monument to the Revolution at Berlin's Friedrichsfelde Central Cemetery, designed by architect Ludwig Mies van der Rohe and inaugurated on June 13, 1926.

Christian Kühn

The Crisis of *Criticality*: Becoming Critically Projective

How can architecture, an artistic practice that depends more than any other on money and power, claim to be critical? In the early 2000s, the concept of *criticality*, that finds its early formulation in K. Michael Hays's text *Critical Architecture: Between Culture and Form* (1984) came under attack from a younger generation of architects and theorists who regarded it as "obsolete, irrelevant and/or as inhibiting design creativity."[1] In the 2002 polemic, published in *A+U* under the title "Design Intelligence," Michael Speaks distances himself from a series of tendencies he perceives as obsolete. As he writes, "Post-modernism, Deconstructivism, Critical Regionalism and a host of other critical architectures in the late 1980s and 1990s posed [...] as false pretenders to Modernism. [...] Stuck between a world of certainty whose demise they had been instrumental in bringing about, and an emergent world of uncertainty into which they were being thrown headlong, these theoretical vanguards were incapacitated by their own resolute negativity."[2]

Resistance and negation, which, according to Speaks, were at the core of these vanguards, simply made no sense anymore. Striving for an architecture "no longer under man's control," as Peter Eisenman, one of the key figures of that vanguard, proposes, seemed awkward in a world that could not be controlled anyway, as it was subject to the erratic development of the globalized economy and the new distribution of political and military power. It is not by chance that the discussion on criticality started in the context of the burst of the dot-com bubble and 9/11.

As a way out of this uncomfortable situation, Michael Speaks proposes *design intelligence*, thus alluding to the meaning of *intelligence* in the context of secret service activities. Instead of being entrapped in their formal, theoretical, or professional identities, the designers following this new post-vanguard idea of design would be "accustomed [...] to open source intelligence (OSINT as it is called by the CIA) gathered from the little truths published on the web, found in popular culture, and gleaned from other professions and design disciplines."[3] These new practices would be "adaptable to almost any circumstance almost everywhere."[4]

The merit of giving this approach a catchy name goes to Sarah Whiting and Robert Somol, who, at that time, taught at Harvard and UCLA, respectively. In their text under the hermetical title "Notes around the Doppler Effect and other Moods of Modernism," published in *Perspecta* in 2002, they propose a *projective* architectural practice focusing on performance and efficacy.[5] Rather than looking back and criticizing the status quo, this practice projects forward alternative arrangements and scenarios, which are not necessarily oppositional. The link to the contemporary Dutch architecture is obvious, and it is no coincidence that Michael Speaks was one of its major promoters in the US. Rem Koolhaas's remark on the subject, in its most condensed form, predates the discussion in the US by almost a decade:

> "We have to imagine 1001 other concepts of the city, we have to take insane risks, we have to dare to be utterly uncritical [...] Since we are not responsible, we have to become irresponsible."[6]

In retrospect, one may argue whether a *projective turn* in architecture has actually occurred. Certainly, market orientation and a focus on efficacy are uncritically endorsed by the mainstream architectural practices today. A 'turn,' however, would have equipped us with a theory of this projective practice, a set of tools that would allow us to navigate the world of the "insane risks" that Koolhaas refers to. In an early analysis of the *projective*, published in the Harvard Design magazine in 2004, George Baird calls exactly for this:

> "It is clear that a new projective architecture will not be able to be developed in the absence of a supporting body of projective theory. Without it, I predict that this new architecture will devolve to the 'merely' pragmatic, and to the 'merely' decorative, with astonishing speed."[7]

Baird goes on to question the extent to which "the putatively 'projective' forms of practice being advocated by the new critics of criticality will develop parallel models of critical assessment with which to be able to measure the ambition and the capacity for significant social transformation of such forms."[8] In Baird's view, a *projective turn* would have to be accompanied by a renewed critical practice going beyond resistance and negativity as its main tactics.

In search of a foundation of such a practice, it is worth referring back to Hays's "Critical Architecture: Between Culture and Form," the text that Somol and Whiting call "canonical."[9] For the latter, Hays's argument boils down to the idea of resistance by negativity, which he prominently exemplifies through Ludwig Mies van der Rohe's practice.[10] However, in my reading, Hays's argument is much broader, offering alternative options of an architectural practice between culture and form that may reconcile the critical with the projective.

As the subtitle of Hays's text indicates, he explores the tension between culture and form for both the production and reception of architecture. At the extremes of this field of tension, architecture is reduced either to an epiphenomenon of culture or to an autonomous formal system that can be investigated regardless of the conditions of its formation. Hays sets his agenda with a clear problem statement:

> "In this essay, I shall examine a critical architecture, one resistant to the self-confirming, conciliatory operations of a dominant culture and yet irreducible to a purely formal structure disengaged from the contingencies of place and time."[11]

Hays first sets out to review these two prevalent interpretative perspectives. The first position emphasizes culture as the cause and content of built form, and defines the task of the interpreter as "the study of objects and environments as signs, symptoms, and instruments of cultural values."[12] When the cultural situation in which the object originates is correctly reconstructed, "an 'objective and true' explanation of the object in question results."[13] The opposite position renunciates the idea of a "single 'truth,' and advocates a proliferation of interpretations based solely on form."[14] Architectural form is conceived as a product of a certain time and place, but "the origin of the object is not allowed to constrain its meaning."[15] Hays concedes that this approach has its benefits: it has done away with "testimonials proclaiming a work's greatness and humanistic worth on the basis of its accurate representation of the dominant culture."[16] Nevertheless, proclaiming the absolute autonomy of form and its superiority over historical and material contingencies comes with a price: "Reduced to pure form, architecture has disarmed itself from the start, maintaining its purity by acceding to social and political inefficacy."[17]

Hays proposes an alternative position that cuts across this dichotomy by accepting architectural objects as always situated "explicitly and critically *in the world* — in culture, in theories of culture, in theories of interpretation itself."[18] This position requires a more intricate analysis of the object as "historical contingency, as well as the artefact's persistent sensuous particularity, must all be considered as incorporated in the architectural object."[19]

Being situated explicitly and critically in the world is the essence of Hays's proposal for a new positioning of the architectural object between culture and form. Why he goes on to exemplify this idea through a series of projects that Ludwig Mies van der Rohe designed between 1919 and 1929 is not exactly clear to the reader, and even less clear is the text's conclusion that critical architecture can only be realized by the very attitude of silence and negation, which Hays observes in Mies's architecture. Let us first have a brief look at these projects. The first two are the famous high-rise projects for Berlin, Friedrichstraße (1919, 1922), which Hays analyzes in relation to the condition of the metropolis in the early 20th century. While the 1919 high-rise, with its crystalline shape, is still organized hierarchically as parts composing a larger whole, the 1922 project, with its curved surfaces, is conceived as an unarticulated "unitary volume that does not permit itself to be read in terms of an internal formal logic."[20] For Hays, this is the perfect representation of the human condition in the metropolis as described by other authors of the time, such as Georg Simmel. "The convex, faceted surfaces are perceptually contorted by the invasion of circumstantial images, while the reflection each concavity receives on its surface is that of its own shadow, creating gaps which exacerbate the disarray."[21] This reading of the building's appearance is well supported by a charcoal drawing of the tower's shaft by Mies, which shows a random array of vertical lines rising up from the ground. It is the sense of surface and volume, severed from the knowledge of any internal order or logic "that wrenches the building from the atemporal, idealized realm of autonomous form and installs it in a specific situation in the real world of experienced time [...]."[22]

Hays claims to find the same qualities in Mies's 1928 project for Alexanderplatz in Berlin. In a radical contrast to the original urban setting, which would lend itself to a circular composition, the blocks and slabs of the project are placed with hardly any reference neither to the place nor to each other. Nevertheless, for Hays, they convey meaning by their very negation of any easily comprehensible formal logic.

> "Mies's achievement was to open a clearing of implacable silence in the chaos of the nervous metropolis, this clearing is a radical critique, not only of the established spatial order of the city and the established logic of classical composition, but also of the inherent *nervenleben*."[23]

Mies's architecture became critical by distinguishing itself from the forces that influence architecture — the conditions established by the market and by taste, the personal aspirations of its author, its technical origins, even its purpose. To achieve this, Mies, according to Hays, rendered his architecture in "implacable silence" and placed it at the very position "between culture as a massive body of self-perpetuating ideas and form supposedly free of circumstance."[24] The idea of "implacable silence" can hardly be applied to another work of Mies from the same period: the Barcelona pavilion that opened in 1929. Hays concedes that this building is full of references, a synthesis of Wright's horizontal planes and the abstract compositions "of the Suprematists-Elementarists, with honorific nods to the walls of Berlage, [...] the materials of Loos, and the podium and column of Schinkel, all processed through the spatial conceptions of de Stijl."[25] But this, he claims, was not Mies's intention. What looks rational and clear from a distance dissolves when the visitor approaches and enters the enclosed spaces. In Hays's reading, Mies created a surrealistic space full of reflections and illusions without any prescribed logic of passage, an assemblage of different parts of disparate materials.

> "Because there is no conceptual center to organize the parts or transcend pure perception of them, the particular quality of each material is registered as a kind of absolute."[26]

Space is fragmented and distorted, with any overarching logic of space and time systematically dispersed. "The work itself is an event with temporal duration, whose actual existence is continually being produced."[27] The artefact is nothing less than a "winning of reality," a phrase that Hays borrows from Stanford Andersen.[28] Though existing to a considerable extent by virtue of its formal structures, it cannot be apprehended only formally, nor does it represent a pre-existing reality. "The architectural reality takes its place *alongside* the real world."[29] Thus, the architectural world shares temporal and spatial conditions with the real one, while obstructing its absolute authority. For Hays, the Barcelona pavilion "tears a cleft in the continuous surface of reality."[30]

How does Hays's interpretation of the Barcelona pavilion as "fragmented and distorted" connect with the "implacable silence" of the Alexanderplatz project designed just one year earlier? For Hays, the shared quality is resistance against both the self-confirming operations of the dominant culture and the tendency to reduce architecture to the purely formal, disengaged from the contingencies of place and time. Strangely, Hays does not regard his examples — the Friedrichstraße high-rise, the Barcelona Pavillion and the Alexanderplatz project — as different yet equally effective approaches to criticality, but he reads the history of Mies's work backwards, reducing them to merely a prelude to the "American" Mies of the IIT campus and his later high-rise buildings. Thus, he overlooks a prime example of resistance and critique in Mies's work that predates the Barcelona Pavilion by four years: the monument to Rosa Luxemburg and Karl Liebknecht (1926). During the McCarthy era in the 1950s, Mies had to explain his involvement with the Communist Party of Germany in connection with this project. He remembered being presented with the original project for the monument by a prospective client, Eduard Fuchs, a member of the Communist Party. Referring to the Doric columns of the project, Mies ridiculed them as a "fine monument to a banker," and offered to develop a design of his own, together with the sculptor Herbert Garbe.[31]

Positioning oneself as the architect of this monument was a political statement not without risk. It may suffice to mention that no company was willing to produce the five-pointed stainless-steel star, the symbol of the communist Spartacus League, placed prominently in front of the monument. Eventually, five rhomboids had to be ordered and placed together as a star. The *leitmotif* of the monument is resistance against gravity. The wall dissolves into blocks that are composed of smaller units: the used bricks that, due to the small budget, Mies chose as the cladding material for the concrete structure. The wall's elements start to float at various levels of detail, a seemingly abstract composition that is thoughtfully connected to the everyday by a set of small steps that lead up to a platform in front of the star.

The monument was torn down by the Nazis in 1933. Mies opposed several attempts to reconstruct it after the war, and he probably would have opposed the reconstruction of his Barcelona pavilion too, as both are examples of the architectural positions he distanced himself from. In terms of architectural historiography though, this does not diminish their value. Even if, for the "American" Mies, negativity and silence seemed the last possible form of criticality and resistance, he still had successfully explored other forms in his earlier career. Designing a monument for two murdered revolutionaries in the context of the Weimar Republic was undoubtedly a move of resistance, which he took as an opportunity to critically explore new forms of monumentality. The Barcelona Pavilion, even if, at first glance, it may appear to be an incarnation of the formalisms of modern architecture of the time, can be read, as Hays convincingly proposes, as a radical step beyond, as a fragmented and distorted space systematically dispersing any overarching logic of space and time, as "a cleft in the continuous surface of reality."[32] This is critical architecture, yet one that is built not on silence and negativity, but on a sophisticated spatial regime and numerous allusions.

These projects should suffice to support the idea that *criticality* does not need to be reduced to a radical denial of communication by silence and negativity, as the advocates of the *projective* maintain in their denunciation of *criticality*. With its etymology from the Greek word *krinein*, criticality means simply to make or identify a difference. If a *projective* practice of architecture is the practice of projecting forward alternative arrangements and scenarios, the core of such a practice is making a difference. Thus, projective architecture cannot exist without criticality not only toward the goals of its clients but also toward itself. According to Hays, the responsibility of architectural criticism is "to concentrate on the intrinsic conditions through which architecture is made possible."[33] As architectural criticism and critical historiography are "practices continuous with architectural design," the individual consciousness of the architect "is part of and is aware of the collective historical and social situation. Because of this awareness, the individual is not a mere product of the situation but is an historical and social actor in it. There is choice and therefore the responsibility of critical architecture."[34]

Unless architecture today wants to see itself completely instrumentalized by neo-liberal interests and constraints, it needs to develop a *critically projective* practice, which likely needs equally as much self-criticism and the ability to critically evaluate the intrinsic conditions that make a specific project possible. This practice might have to disguise itself as cynicism (as in Rem Koolhaas' invitation to become utterly uncritical) or as naiveté (as in Bjarke Ingels proposition of a pragmatic utopianism). But behind that disguise the goal is the same: positioning architecture explicitly and critically *in the world*, at the right point between culture and form.

1 George Baird, "'Criticality' and Its Discontents," *Harvard Design Magazine*, no. 21 (Fall 2004/Winter 2005). → http://www.harvarddesignmagazine.org/issues/21/criticality-and-its-discontents
2 Michael Speaks, "Design Intelligence: Part 1, Introduction," *A+U: Architecture and Urbanism* 12, no. 387 (2002): 10—18.
3 Ibid.
4 Ibid.
5 Robert Somol and Sarah Whiting, "Notes Around the Doppler Effect and Other Moods of Modernism," *Perspecta* 33 (2002): 72—77.
6 O.M.A., Rem Koolhaas, and Bruce Mau, *S, M, L, XL* (New York: The Monacelli Press, 1995), 971.
7 Baird.
8 Ibid.
9 Somol and Whiting, 73.
10 Ibid.
11 K. Michael Hays, "Critical Architecture: Between Culture and Form," *Perspecta* 21 (1984): 15.
12 Hays, 16.
13 Ibid.
14 Ibid.
15 Ibid.
17 Hays, 17.
18 Ibid.
19 Ibid.
20 Hays, 19.
21 Ibid.
22 Hays, 20.
23 Hays, 22.
24 Ibid.
25 Ibid.
26 Hays, 24.
27 Ibid.
28 Hays, 29, Footnote 12.
29 Hays, 25.
30 Ibid.
31 Neue Gesellschaft für Bildende Kunst, *Wem gehört die Welt?* (Berlin, 1977).
32 Hays, 25.
33 Hays, 27.
34 Ibid.

Ana Jeinić

From Non-Projective Criticality toward a Radical Critical Projectivity: Design in the Age of Speculations

Paradoxical logic of critical architecture as pursuit of *non-projective projects*

Although Robert Somol and Sarah Whiting's article "Notes around the Doppler Effect and Other Moods of Modernism" from 2002 received much attention within the architectural discourse of the following years, it somehow went unnoticed that the notion of *projective architecture*, which constituted the conceptual core of Somol and Whiting's argument, was, in fact, a pleonasm.[1] Considering that the (architectural) project has served as the central instrument and final outcome of architectural design at the latest since architecture was established as an independent discipline in the Renaissance, deploying the term *projective* to denote a particular approach to design is not much different than it would be to describe a specific sort of literature as *textual*. Thus, the usage of the term *projective architec-*

ture, if it is not to be understood as a pure tautology, implies the existence of an architectural practice that is not projective and that therefore contradicts the century-long idea of architecture as a discipline. Since "Notes about the Doppler Effect" was constructed around the opposition between projective and *critical* architecture, we must assume that it is within this latter category where the deviant, non-projective projects are to be found. This leads us to the second remarkable implication of Somol and Whiting's thesis — not only that it presupposes a weird form of design that can be described only by an oxymoron (the *non-projective project*), but also that this paradoxical way of practicing architecture is labeled *critical*, which implies that architectural design can be *either* projective *or* critical (and not projective *and* critical at the same time).

In the years after the essay was published, several architectural theorists proved that not only the specific arguments of its authors, but also the broader discursive field in which it was situated — the field constituted by the debate between *critical* and *post-critical* interpretations of the social role of architectural design — was questionable in many respects.[2] Firstly, it was shown that the very concept of the critique (and of architecture's capacity of being critical) that was shared by both the generation of "critical" architects of the 1970s—1980s and the subsequent generation of their "post-critical" opponents was rather problematic, being a product of a particular (and in itself contradictory) lineage of the theory development.[3] Secondly, the term *projective architecture*, introduced as the antipode to this particular idea of *critical architecture*, was itself debunked as vague, ambiguous, and incapable of achieving much more than to provide an additional intellectual legitimization to those practices that, in line with the general neoliberal climate of the 1990s and early 2000s, deprived architecture of *any* (however conceived) critical aspirations and took an utterly pragmatic approach instead.[4]

Considering that the terms *critical* and *projective architecture* have all but disappeared from the contemporary architectural discourse as a result of the above-exposed countermining insights, it might seem somewhat anachronistic to revert to these concepts now, fifteen years after "Notes about the Doppler Effect" was published. However, even though I agree that the *criticality* vs. *post-criticality* debate and the seminal texts through which it was brought about represented a dead end in the development of the architectural theory, it seems to me, nevertheless, that there was something more at stake in the unwitting paradoxes of Somol and Whiting's essay than just the unfortunate deployment of the terms *critical* and *projective*. More precisely, the contradictions apparent in the text might lead us to asking fundamental questions regarding the agency of architecture, questions that in view of the rampant *uncritical projectivity* characterizing the contemporary construction industry, financial practices, logistic systems, and other determinant factors in the production of the built environment could be even more relevant today than they were fifteen years ago.

What actually is *project*?

Seen in the context of (architectural) design, *project* can be understood as an instrument through which the activity of *designing* is carried out, formalized, and represented, be it in the form of textual descriptions, drawings, diagrams, or 3D models. However, this definition alone does not tell us much about the nature of project-making except for pointing to the fact that, in the context of design disciplines, *project* and *design* are two closely related — and in most cases mutually interchangeable — concepts. So, what then is *design*? Herbert A. Simon defined it famously: "Everyone designs who devises courses of action aimed at changing existing situations into preferred ones."[5] If we strip this definition of Simon's overtly scientistic, cybernetic, and solutions-oriented theoretical construct, it can serve as a broad and preliminary explanation of what designing (that is, *making design projects*) is about, or, more precisely, what it *was* about in the modern era, which brought about both the design disciplines in their contemporary sense and the very idea of *project* in its conventional meaning.

The above-quoted definition is useful because its simplicity enables us to immediately identify the two principal aspects and the related temporal structure of the practice of design. The "preferred situations" mentioned in the definition point to the self-evident fact that every design project has a future-oriented aspect that can be called *projective* or *speculative*. To explain it in simple words: every project is *projective* insofar as it contains the imaginative construction (*projection*) of a not-yet-existent but possible—and, in the view of the designer, *preferable*—future situation. Yet there is a second aspect of design, which, even though not so apparent, is implied in Simon's definition—before the "existing situations" are turned into the "preferred ones," the designer must assess them critically (that is, make *critical judgments* about them) in order to know what and why needs to be changed. This second, implicit component of a project, which is related to the agency of *reflection* and oriented toward the *present* and the *past*, can be called *critical*. Seen from this perspective, every project unifies the *projective* with the *critical* agency, and the *speculative* construction of the future with the *reflexive* assessment of the present (including the past developments, inscribed in the present situation). However, this abstract designation of (architectural) projects as *critically projective* conceptual devices is still useless for understanding the concrete potentials of architectural agency within a broader social context—that is, the factual meaning of architectural "criticality" and "projectivity." Thus, what needs to be examined next is *in what sense* and *by what means* architectural projects can be critical and/or projective.

The critique implied in architectural projects can be manifold (in terms of object, scale, and art of criticism), and it depends on the concrete form that this immanent critique assumes whether a project really deserves to be called critical in any meaningful sense of the term. Thus, the "existing situation" can be critically evaluated by the designer in purely technical or managerial terms, in which case it does not make much sense to speak of a properly critical design. However, the implicit critique expressed by a project can go beyond practical concerns and refer as well to cultural, ecological, economic, political, or other aspects of the environment, or to the "internal" architectural issues reaching from form-related questions, to specific design methodologies, all the way to the conceptual foundations of the discipline. The "level" of criticism can also differ—the existing situation can be assessed on the basis of the existing value systems, but designers can question value systems as well, which brings their critical assessments to the level of *systemic critique*.

The ways in which design can be projective are as manifold as the ways in which it can be critical. As I have already outlined, projectivity refers to *futureness* (that is, to the immanent forward-looking aspect) of projects. As conceptual constructions of not-yet-existing realities, projects are characterized by a *speculative temporality*. This means that in the course of designing critical assessments of the present are turned into proposals for the future, which are then projected back to the present, informing our actions directed toward the realization of the envisaged future situation. The time span between the present moment and the "projected" future can, however, vary greatly: from projects that are realized simultaneously when being developed, to the common architectural designs (which generally require several months or several years to bc materialized), all the way to so called paper architectures, which depict a possible future horizon without specifying the time frame of its realization. In the majority of cases, there is a correlation between the project's time frame and the grade of the difference between the present situation and the imaginary one conceived by the designer; the difference between the *now* (of the present reality) and the *then* (of the project) tends to be bigger for the projects with an extended time frame. The projects envisaging situations that are substantially different from the present reality (and, consequently, unlikely to be realized in a near future) can be termed *visionary*.

A further differentiation regarding the projective component of design is related to the nature of the critique that is implicitly exerted by means of a project. In other words, the scope and kind of the projective imagination will vary depending on the scope and kind of the critical assessment inherent in a project. Thus, if the critical assessment is of a purely technical nature, so will be the design. If, on the other hand, the critique concerns broader issues and assumes systemic features, the design is also likely to achieve a more radical level of the projective vision. Projects that are based on a socially relevant critique, develop systemic alternatives, and have extended or unspecified time frames can be considered *utopian*. This means that utopian projects carry *both* the critical and projective components of design to the extreme, thereby being simultaneously critical (in the socially relevant sense of that term) *and* visionary.

The awkward divorce between critical and projective components of design

If the notions of *critical*, *visionary*, and *utopian architecture* are defined as I have proposed — that is, in regard to the radicality of the critical and projective component of design — there should not be much doubt that the history of modern architecture abounds in projects of all the three sorts. Even though the term *critical architecture* was not frequently in use until the crisis of modernity in the late 20th century, we can retroactively deploy it to describe the design strategy and associated projects that, being mostly in direct or indirect connection with a *reformist* social agenda, took a critical stance on the existing built environment and proposed concrete measures for its betterment; the examples thereof reach from model housing, a garden city movement, and other initiatives for the betterment of the dwelling conditions of the working class in the 19th century, to the modern housing estates and urban developments enabled by the social-democratic governments and progressive industrialists of the inter-war years, to the socially-informed modernism of the post-war Keynesian era.[6] On the other hand, the term *visionary architecture* (denoting projects with the strong projective and moderate critical dimension) is suitable for describing the designs that demonstrated exceptionally high levels of technical, formal, or methodological inventiveness in the way they depicted possible futures, although they were not necessarily related to a fundamental critique of the present (Richard Buckminster Fuller's innovative ideas and constructions provide a vivid example). Different from the pragmatic reformist critique and apolitical visionary speculations, *uto-*

pian projects were mostly connected to radical political agendas, as they proposed *systemic alternatives* based on *systemic critique* (Constant Nieuwenhuys' *New Babylon* is one of the most manifest examples).

Even such brief and superficial observations regarding the *critical*, *visionary*, and *utopian* architectures of the modern era suffice for concluding that modern design strategies that could be meaningfully assigned to any of these categories always retained the conceptual structure of a project implied in Herbert A. Simon's definition: they were concerned with the *betterment* of existing situations and thus were simultaneously critical *and* projective (even though the critical component sometimes prevailed over the projective one and vice versa). This brings us back to one of the initial concerns of this essay — something must have changed at the end of the 20th century, enabling the dissolution of the internal composition of the modern project and the resulting separation between the notions of the *critical* and the *projective* in the context of architectural design. Beyond some specific developments of architectural discourse and practice (the analysis of which would go beyond the scope of this text), several factors that played a role in the peculiar detachment of the critical from the projective dimension of design were related to a general shift in the dominant political model and intellectual climate that occurred in the last decades of the century.

In the 1970s and 1980s, the hostility toward comprehensive economic planning, which characterized the ascending neoliberal doctrine, converged with the critique of the state bureaucracy expressed by the revolting left in the previous decade,[7] while the collapsing Soviet project encouraged the view that there existed an intrinsic link between utopian projects and totalitarian regimes. Simultaneously, the post-structuralist discourse dominating the humanities in the last decades of the 20th century required that intellectuals (including "intellectual architects") engage in endless circles of deconstruction of dominant discourses, while prohibiting them to propose any alternatives since such *projections* would be seen as yet another act of fixation of meaning and, consequently, of domination.[8] As a result of these tendencies, architects (particularly those associated with high-profile academic institutions) developed implicit disrespect for what was for centuries considered the defining feature of design: its *projectivity*. They started treating architectural projects as tools for the explicit "critical" interpretation and "deconstruction" of inherited design formulas instead of using it for an affirmative anticipation of the future. This attitude provoked a rebellious reaction of a younger generation of theorists and practitioners, who turned away from the "critical" and embraced once again the "projective" approach. They maintained, however, the fundamental assumption implicit in the work of their antecedents — the belief that the projective dimension of architecture is always compromised by and subservient to the dominant social forces, and, in consequence, incompatible with any serious critical ambitions.[9] In effect, this meant that those who wanted to be "projective" had no other option than consciously and voluntarily *surf the waves of capitalism*. Thus, the radical *critical projectivity* characterizing the utopian ethos of the 1960s and 1970s was equally deprecated by both "critical" *and* "projective" (or "post-critical") architects of the late 20th and early 21st century.

(Non-projective) reflexivity in contemporary architecture and its limits

After the basic premises of the polarization between "critical" and "projective" architecture had come under suspicion, both terms (particularly the latter one) quickly lost much of their erstwhile popularity. This, however, did not signal the comeback of the *utopian design* in the sense in which I have defined it before (i.e. as the strategy unifying radical critique with radical projectivity) because the critical social forces, including architects in their ranks, remained for a long time rather hostile toward the rampant projective imagination and the related speculative approach.[10] Being projective — that is, engaging with the *future* — was disqualified as a dirty job of financial speculators and corporate investors, supported by uncritical, technophile designers, whereas the oppositional left and the "leftist architects" embraced the task of providing critical reflection upon the dominant social tendencies (along with their spatial manifestations) and of experimenting with ad hoc alternative socio-spatial practices. In other words, the left voluntarily limited itself to the past-oriented (*critical reflection*) and present-oriented (*ad hoc experimentation*) forms of agency, while continuing to dismiss the future-oriented speculations.

The result of the tendencies is that even though Somol and Whiting's terminology was largely abandoned by the subsequent generation of architectural theorists and practitioners, the differentiation between the past- and present-oriented modes of architectural practice on the one hand and the future-oriented ones on the other, as well as the disentanglement of the latter from the agency of critique, has been tacitly maintained up to the present day. The context has changed, however, and so have both the character of design strategies associated with diverse temporal models and the names applied to them. Thus, while the term *critical architecture* has been somewhat reluctantly and cautiously used throughout the last two decades, it has found a rather "neutral" and less pretentious substitute in the notion of *reflexive design*, which owes some of its popularity to the recent debates around the distinctiveness and potentials of the *design as research*.[11]

Contemporary architectural studios and groups whose practice has been frequently attributed the quality of pronounced reflexivity (the Berlin-based studio Kuehn Malvezzi being a case in point)[12] have something in common with Eisenman's generation of "critical architects," the distinctive feature of their work is that it enhances the design's criticality/reflexivity, while simultaneously mitigating its projectivity.[13] In this way, the primary scope of an architectural project is removed from envisaging the future and toward revealing, interpreting, questioning, deconstructing, recombining, or reframing what is either considered *absolute* (that is, *timeless*) or what has been handed down from the past (in terms of, be it, the inherited design methodologies and common formal solutions or the preserved built environment). Thus, both the current tendency of highlighting the reflexive dimension of design and the late 20th-century concept of *critical architecture* refer to a type of architectural practice characterized by a rather cautious stance (if not by outright disinterest) when it comes to envisaging how our future dwellings, settlements, and infrastructure might function, what kind of communities, institutions, and practices they might accommodate, how we might live in them, and what ideas and values they should embody.

The described voluntary moderation of the future-oriented dimension of architectural design poses a serious limit to its social relevance, even in case when the critical/reflexive content of the respective projects goes beyond the narrowly defined architectural concerns (formal, constructive, or typological) to address a wider social dimension of the built environment. Limitations to the social efficacy of "reflexive design" are exacerbated by the fact that the *anti-futurist* attitude of its proponents stands in stark contrast to the highly speculative logic of investors, real estate agents, financial enterprises, futures traders, insurance companies, police and military strategists, developers of *smart technologies*, and other actors who exert decisive influence upon the present-day production and management of space. Needless to say, these speculative practices (which not only increasingly determine our future but also recursively affect our present) generally result not from critical reflexions upon the present condition of the built environment but rather from motives related to pursuing individual profit or achieving specific goals by means of preemptive action.[14] Thus, the living conditions of the majority are increasingly dependent on the pragmatic speculative calculus of the few, making the *utopian counter-speculation* (i.e. the imaginative construction of alternative futures based on the systemic critique of the present) more needed than ever. It is for this reason that the reflexive tendencies in the contemporary architectural practice cannot contribute much to emancipatory socio-spatial transformations as long as they refuse to translate the critical reflection upon *the existing* into projective visions of *the possible.*

Reclaiming the *critical projectivity* of design

The detached reflexivity relating to the "conceptualist" and "contextualist" tendencies in contemporary design, is, however, not the only strategy that characterizes the work of architects interested in broadening the scope of their practice beyond the merely pragmatic and aesthetic concerns. Arguably, the majority of designers aspiring to reclaim the social relevance and transformative potential of the discipline have adopted, in the course of the last two decades, the approach described alternately by terms such as *activist*, *tactical*, *militant*, or *guerrilla design*. Different from the "reflexive strategy," this approach keeps a project's critical/reflexive component implicit, in line with the conventional understanding of design. Here too, however, the critique of the present is *not* transformed into the projection of a (different) future, but, in this case, into the immediate, present-oriented action. The common result is temporary urban interventions and ephemeral spatial constructions that embody the preference for *local* scale, *present* moment, *loose* connections, *instable* organizational patterns, and *reactive* (rather than projective) forms of engagement characterizing the contemporary (leftist) political activism.[15]

In the last few years, the described trend has been counteracted by the concept formation and practical experimentation in the area of *speculative design*, whose very name is a testimony to the renewed interest in the projective aspect of the design practice.[16] Yet, even though this tendency might point to the direction of the much needed reintegration of the critical and projective dimension of architecture, there is still a certain hesitation when it comes to deploying design as a form of radical, comprehensive, and *utopian* form of imagination — that is, as one which, according to the previously formulated definition, would translate systemic critique into systemic projects. There are several reasons for this hesitation, the first of which lies in the fact that not all proponents of the concept of speculative design identify with the radical political agenda. Further reasons, which, unlike the former, can be theoretically discussed and eventually disarmed, are linked to the negative connotations still clinging to the notion of (architectural) utopianism.

One such negative association impeding the emphatic resumption of utopian design stems from the claim that utopian prospects formulated by designers can only anticipate the emerging forms of the capitalist economic and political organization, yet would never point toward an altogether different (non-capitalist) future.[17] This claim, justified by architecture's supposedly unavoidable subservience to the process of capital accumulation, overlooks, however, the emancipatory potential residing in the speculative temporality of architectural projects. Whereas the thesis on the inextricable relation between architecture and capital might indeed hold for the projects that are realized within the conventional, narrow time-frame of the building industry and are entrapped in the corresponding relation between the client (as the capital provider) and the architect (as the service provider), it does not make much sense for the *truly* utopian projects that address time-scales exceeding ones typical of commercial design tasks.

A further negative connotation adhering to the notion of a utopian project originates in the supposed link between utopias and violence. There are two basic versions of the argument claiming that utopias are intrinsically violent. The first one is based on the assumption that it lies in the nature of utopianism that the authors and supporters of a utopian project will strive to impose *their* picture of a better future on everyone else, including those for whom that same picture might embody everything negative and undesired.[18] The second version assumes that utopias are static visions of supposedly ideal societies, which, if materialized, must be preserved in their original shape, the usage of violence is thus required as a means of prohibiting all eventual deviations from that (allegedly perfect) form and norm.[19] From a strictly logical point of view, both arguments are correct, but they are presupposed on very narrow definitions of utopianism. They conceive utopias as complete manuals for a one-to-one realization of a social order that is considered perfect by utopia's authors and supporters. However, a utopian project can mean something quite different from such narrowing assumptions.

First, it needs to be pointed out that utopian projects can be voluntarily conceived as open and dynamic prospects. In other words, if a design translates a systemic critique of the present into a systemic proposal of an alternative future (which I have proposed as the condition for a project to be considered utopian), this does not imply that the envisaged future situation is necessarily perceived by a project's authors as an *ideal* one! The utopian design could and *should* rather be understood in the sense proposed by Eduardo Galeano in his famous verse about utopia. For Galeano, utopia is a horizon that always moves away as we try to approach it.[20] The main point here is not that utopias are in principle unattainable (and consequently useless), but that each step toward a utopia faces us with new questions and dilemmas arising from the materialization of the utopian proposal. Therefore, utopian projects need to be constantly reformulated on the way of their realization. In other words, every (utopian) design must be open for endless possibilities of its future *redesign*.[21]

Furthermore, to the same extent that political programs and socially relevant decisions can be arrived at through *dialogical* procedures (i.e. through a collective discourse), so can utopian projects too be appropriated, discussed, and further developed by a broader public. If understood in this way, utopias could function in a way similar to open software — that is, like sketches open for further elaboration, discussion, and contestation. The comparison with open software is also helpful because it points to the fact that for (open) utopian projects to develop their full potential as dynamic objects of exercise in collective imagination, it requires a broad platform of actors interested in appropriating, extending, and redesigning the initial proposal. In other words, if a utopian project is to become a collective project, it needs a *utopian culture*. Thus, the future of utopianism does not depend just on utopian designers, but, primarily, on the willingness of egalitarian social movements to switch from a predominantly *reactive* to predominantly *projective* mode of engagement, since a proper utopian culture can thrive only within the latter mode.

After elevating a utopian project to the level of global political practice, we could reasonably ask ourselves what such broadly defined utopianism has to do with architecture and what role architects might play in developing collective utopias. There are several features of architectural profession that make the participation of architects and other designers in collaborative practices of future-oriented imagination particularly important. First of all, as the above-analyzed definition by Herbert A. Simon shows, designers are, by the very nature of their practice, trained to translate critical assessments of the present into projects for the future. Secondly, design functions as an interface between technological inventions and their social appropriation. Architecture and urban planning, in particular, *socialize* and *spatialize* technology (i.e. they turn it into socially available and spatially accommodated *infrastructure*). Thirdly, as design disciplines generally privilege the visual over textual modes of project development and representation, architects master the tools enabling to translate abstract utopian models into concrete pictures of how we might live in the future so that they can give utopias the shape of concrete, imaginable, and accessible proposals. Considering all this, we can conclude that constructing organizational settings and testing work procedures that will allow a new productive encounter between (utopian) architecture and (utopian) politics presents an extraordinarily important task for both architects/designers aiming to improve the social relevance of their engagement and emancipatory political blocs aspiring to play a major role in shaping the future. In this light, there are only two options for critical architecture in the age of speculations — to become radically projective or to remain sorely irrelevant!

1 Robert Somol and Sarah Whiting, "Notes around the Doppler Effect and Other Moods of Modernism," *Perspecta* 33 (2002): 72—77.
2 See, for example, George Baird, "'Criticality' and its Discontents," *Harvard Design Magazine* 21 (Fall 2004/ Winter 2005): 16—21, and Reinhold Martin, "Critical of What? Toward a Utopian Realism," *Harvard Design Magazine* 22 (Spring/Summer 2005): 104—109.
3 See Martin, "Critical of What?"
4 Ibid.
5 Herbert A. Simon, *The Sciences of the Artificial* (1969, 3rd edition, Cambridge, Massachusetts/London, England: MIT Press, 1996), 111.
6 For the relationship between reformism and critique as exemplified in architectural and urban design, see Tahl Kaminer, *The Efficacy of Architecture. Political Contestation and Agency* (Oxon/New York: Routledge, 2017), 17—52.
7 For this convergence and its consequences for architecture, see Tahl Kaminer, *Architecture, Crisis and Resuscitation. The Reproduction of Post-Fordism in Late-Twentieth-Century Architecture* (Oxon/New York: Routledge, 2011), 117—166.
8 For the incorporation of this attitude into the architectural discourse of the late 20th century, see Kaminer, *The Efficacy of Architecture*, 46—52.
9 See Martin, "Critical of What?"
10 A comprehensive and insightful analysis of the hesitation of the contemporary social movements to devise future-oriented projects is provided in: Nick Srnicek and Alex Williams, "Chapter One: Our Political Common Sense. Introducing Folk Politics," in *Inventing the Future. Postcapitalism and a World Without Work* (London/New York: Verso, 2015), 1—43. On the crisis of future-oriented imagination in contemporary architecture, see my essay "Where Have All the Flowers Gone? Architecture After the Future" in *Archifutures Vol. 2: The Studio. A Field Guide to Speculating upon the Future of Architecture*, ed. &beyond (Barcelona: dpr, 2017), 22—37.
11 Indicative in this regard are publications *Reflexives Entwerfen/ Reflexive Design*, ed. Margitta Buchert (Berlin: Jovis, 2014), and *Praktiken reflexiven Entwerfens*, ed. ibid. (Berlin: Jovis, 2016).
12 Beyond Kuehn Malvezzi, reflexive tendencies can be found in the work of various contemporary studios that have tried to escape the market-driven imperatives of the neoliberal building practice by embracing a more "contemplative," "conceptual," "narrative," and/or "contextual" approach to design. As "reflexive architecture" cannot be viewed as a unitary movement, the examples are very heterogeneous, including practices such as Monadnock, Eric Lappiere, Pezo Von Ellrichshausen, Thomas Raynaud Architects, or Dogma. The most radical expression of reflexivity in architecture implies, however, the total renunciation of design's inherent projectivity and the resulting transformation of architectural practice into a purely analytical enterprise (a good example of this is Eyal Weizman's concept of *forensic architecture*, denoting a form of practice in which architectural tools and knowledges are used for revealing hidden agendas and violent events inscribed in the built environment).
13 For this topic, see, for example, my interview with Wilfried Kuehn on the Architecture After the Future Blog, → http://architecture-after-the-future.org/practice/wifried-kuehn-kuehn-malvezzi-architects (accessed January 2018).
14 On the notion of preemption and its ubiquity in the contemporary society, see Armen Avanessian and Suhail Malik, "The Speculative Time-Complex," → http://dismagazine.com/discussion/81924/the-time-complex-postcontemporary (accessed January 2018).
15 For the critical analysis of the instable and present-oriented forms

of political engagement characterizing contemporary left, see, for example: Nick Srnicek and Alex Williams, *Inventing the Future*, §8.1–43; Jodi Dean, *The Communist Horizon* (London/New York: Verso, 2012), 53–69; and Robin Mackay and Armen Avanessian, "Introduction," in *Accelerate. The Accelerationist Reader*, ed. ibid. (Berlin: Merve, 2014), 1–46. For the critical analysis of contemporary architecture's ephemeral, tactical, and localist strategies, see: René Boer and Mark Minkjan, "Why the Pop-up Hype Isn't Going to Save Our Cities," → https://www.failedarchitecture.com/why-the-pop-up-hype-isnt-going-to-save-our-cities (accessed January 2018); Neil Brenner, "Is 'Tactical Urbanism' an Alternative to Neoliberal Urbanism?" → http://post.at.moma.org/content_items/587-is-tactical-urbanism-an-alternative-to-neoliberal-urbanism (accessed January 2018); and Kaminer, *The Efficacy of Architecture*, 65–132.

16 Among the texts and publications concerned with the notion of speculative design, see, for example: Anthony Dunne and Fiona Raby, *Speculative Everything. Design, Fiction, and Social Dreaming* (Cambridge, Massachusetts/London, England: MIT Press, 2013); Ivica Mitrović, Marko Golub, and Oleg Šuran, *Uvod u spekulativnu dizajnersku praksu. Eutropija, studija slucaja/Introduction to Speculative Design Practice.* Eutropia, a Case Study (Zagreb/Split: HDD & DVK UMAS, 2015); Benjamin H. Bratton, "On Speculative Design," → http://dismagazine.com/discussion/81971/on-speculative-design-benjamin-h-bratton (accessed January 2018).

17 This skeptical view can be deduced from the arguments exposed in Manfredo Tafuri's seminal text *Progetto e Utopia. Architettura e sviluppo capitalistico* (1973, repr., Rome–Bari: Laterza, 2007).

18 One of the most concise and influential formulations of this argument is provided in: Karl Popper, "Utopia and Violence" in *Conjectures and Refutations* (1963, repr., London/New York: Routledge, 2002), 477–488.

19 David Harvey analyzes such (static) utopias as a specific utopian type, which he terms "utopias of spatial form." See David Harvey, *Spaces of Hope* (Edinburgh: Edinburgh University Press, 2000), 159–173.

20 Eduardo Galeano, *Las palabras andantes* (Buenos Aires: Catalogos, 2001), 230.

21 The argument for the radical openness of "world-projects" (Weltentwürfe) is concisely formulated in Friedrich von Borries, *Weltentwerfen. Eine politische Designtheorie* (Berlin: Suhrkamp, 2016).

fig. 13 Ruskin Square, Croydon, 2012

"Don't make it sound heroic; that's why, we have put the key-note last."

This text was written after a talk in Vienna in November 2015 for the conference "Critique or Crisis." We took the invitation as an opportunity for a shared critique of muf's practice rather than an invitation as flattery and to think our studio work in relation to our role in a situation as the ones who are paid to be there, and what we do with that privilege.

Since muf started working together in the mid-1990s, we have been trying out ways to expand a project brief in order that it reflects more than the source of funding and the limited indicators of success. This way of working includes the acceptance of compromised briefs and then expanding their scope through a willfully literal interpretation. Often, this also means working for free and then making it sound better by calling it "unsolicited research." So the time-consuming construction to make it more OK to work in a particular setting can exceed in its scale and complexity the built thing itself.[1]

In what follows, muf's work is described as a "ghost of Christmas future"[2]: if you do not protect your civic institutions and public spaces for all ages, you too might have to operate in a landscape such as ours — the UK and specifically London in the 21st century.

Practicing in London

To take a commission in a dodgy situation, which is mostly the case in London now after years of austerity, is a public statement of complicity. Austerity, visibly directed against social housing, civic space, investments for under 5's, children and young people, the old, the poor, the parks, the sites of non-monetary exchange sitting up close with pockets of dramatic real estate investment.

The question: "are you shoring something up rather than resist, march, or tend a garden?" is implicit in choosing to practice. I would argue that it includes also those who describe their practice as critical, alternative, or radical, who also operate within the same system of critique no matter whether they add the words “architecture,” “urbanism,” or “practice.” The areas where you can practice as a counter to the norm remain very limited, just as in the case of law after the erosion of legal aid, the opportunities to commission architects for those without money for fees get less, and the opportunities to work pro bono are equally tricky.[3] There is a danger in the tendency to be ever flexible, ever more creative, in finding a mode of practice in a hostile landscape.

Over the past decades, the UK has seen a wholesale undermining of the public sphere through various forms of privatization. Parks have lost their budgets and are rented out for private events. The same goes for museums, even if they remain free. More and more opportunities for revenue are inserted. Schools have lost their architects and are now built as a kit. Hospitals operate at their limit. And yet, this is not the same type of recession as in the mid-1990s, when muf was first established. Since then, the budgets for all the everyday things, considered essential services, have been cut.

At the same time, the private has been made “more public”: London is rich, and it is philanthropy, which invests in culture, and it is culture, which has been named a producer of wealth in the attempt to justify investment in it. The celebration of the value of public space as a "thing," first promoted by Richard Rogers, was made an ambition in Ken Livingstone’s “100-Public-Spaces” program for London.[4] muf’s Barking Town Square was one of them — the regime changed, but the idea that publicly accessible space should be the by-product of development stuck.

Wedging the Door Open and *Deep Hanging Out*

A considerable body of work in the studio can be summarized by two approaches: 1) making compromises while trying not to be compromised, and 2) staying in the room long enough to wedge the door open for others without an invitation. This description of muf's methodology can easily be found in the public space commissions we have undertaken, such as Barking Town Square, which overtly sits within a larger project driven by other agendas. muf's strategy can be detailed further.

Good work requires a degree of accuracy. But projects for public spaces are usually generic, so the brief remains incomplete. In order to close the distance between the observer and the observed, the architect and—with the broadest possible interpretation of that term—the client, we practice "Deep Hanging Out."[5] The danger for the architect as an "agent of expensiveness"[6] is that this "hanging out" is often more with the developer or the institution than with the user—that is, with the relevant section of the public. So all that is left for us is to make the most of the privilege that our status as commissioned professionals affords us.

We wedge the door open for other people and other agendas so that they can enter and complete the brief in ways that are sometimes obvious and sometimes less so. We describe this as "unsolicited research," the extra work necessary to make a project both meaningful and bearable.

After the Designer leaves, or *Incompleteness*

Successful projects respond to this call to complete an incomplete brief by designing work that is intentionally incomplete, work that is open to appropriation and inhabitation by those who are not in the room. The more careful the surveying of the ground is and the more carefully we get it right through understanding a situation, the better the preparation for the project's *afterlife* gets (that is, its life after the designer leaves).

Incompleteness is a process, which also plays out as formal moves, intentionally specifying the materially luxurious deployed (necessarily given the budgets) unevenly to confer status on the everyday.

At muf, we amass typologies of "incompleteness" open to appropriation, built-out formal moves, as details, as furniture, as suggested uses in the right size for a child but not codified as for children. We make use of familiar forms like the plinth, the monumental, a flight of steps, or the bench. Some examples:

A flight of steps is positioned not as a necessary means to navigate a 3-metre change in level but rather as giving status to a civic space, ceremonial lounging, Marian Court, a mixed tenure housing project for the London Borough of Hackney, or fences and boundaries which invite use rather than repel, Wick Green, or in the space of adults extend an invitation to the child, seat in Ruskin Square, or marking out in terrazzo the profile of one of the churches which once stood on a site in Altab Ali Park, Whitechapel. The central strip is rough on this elevated plane and polished at the edges where one might sit. Part plinth, part path, it becomes the place to line up at midnight, one night of the year on International Language Day, to lay a wreath, a site of protest and somewhere to lounge. This is the description of one element in Altab Ali Park, named after a murdered garment worker, at the site of a former churchyard, the original "White Chapel" and the Shaheed Minar monument to the martyrs for the Bengali language. It was one of a suite of projects that we authored. While the brief asked for way-finding to the Olympic site, we argued for spending of that budget just off-route, recognizing it would be the last public money spent here for a long time.

A major part of muf's work deals with open space that is privately owned yet publicly accessible, most often with developments of mixed tenure housing where local authorities can only build social housing by building private housing to pay for it.

Our contribution is to state an ambition for a ground pane, which is at least 6-meter thick (to include the ground floor of buildings and tree roots) and to collaborate only if we are part of the masterplanning, which draws the first relationship of buildings and open space. A ground floor plan that is blind to the type of tenure — owned, rented, public, private — inside out. It is an example of work which is quite satisfying and worth doing as it demonstrates what is possible and desirable to those who would position social housing round the back with its own poor door and open space.

Wedge One
Ruskin Square: Opening a Door by Degrees

Ruskin Square is a sequence of open spaces between buildings for a new development in Croydon at the very edge of London, which are all accessible to pedestrians. The large development consists of commercial buildings and housing, beside East Croydon train station, through which 24 million people pass each year. A pioneer development site, a 15-minute walk from the development, is called Ruskin Square, named after John Ruskin, although he himself did not live there (his grandmother ran a pub close to the site, and Ruskin paid to have the river there cleaned in memory of his mother). muf were commissioned to design the approach to the public realm, with Foster + Partners having produced the masterplan. They described it as a piece of city, with convincing clear routes opened in spaces to front the proposed buildings, which led, in turn, to the city beyond the site. Those who have worked with Foster + Partners know how skilled they are in maintaining the clarity of their projects and keeping at a distance any kind of interference, be it visual, activity, or aesthetic.

In a property industry, which is inevitably all about limiting risk for investors, the challenge is to find ways to insert the riskiest thing, the unknown, and use itself. The thin end of the wedge in this project was the branding of the site, which predated our commission: *Ruskin Square*.

One technique of the studio is what we call "studied naiveté," a way of holding a brief to account by taking it very seriously, simplistically so. Our first act in wedging the door open was to take phrases from Ruskin's work as justifications for rather intuitive design moves, responding to the long-time frustration of local actors with the mothballing of the site. Ruskin wrote a lot.

One quote from Ruskin — "Life is Wealth"— justified framing the derelict site as a garden. Another one — "a healthy manner of play is necessary for a healthy manner of work" (we too, like the developer, used phrases in isolation) — justified introducing sport facilities. Football did not resonate with the client and their investors, but cricket did. And it was cricket, as we were told, that was played by the young Afghan refugees who were housed in Croydon with foster parents. The temporary garden which the developers funded was beautiful, a path threading as an arc through an overgrown landscape of wild flowers, arriving first at a concrete slab articulated as an outside room and then onto the two over-sized framed practice nets.

The garden was temporary and did establish some ground rules that we were able to push the client to recognize over the seven years since we first received the commission. These ground rules include: the idea that corporate landscapes can host young people, the value of investment in the public realm in advance of the building of new buildings, the juxtaposition of the formal and the wild as a design language, and the Ruskin "brand" as a creative resource, which became a shared reference for us and the client to fall back on, even though we had different motivations. We imagined the final landscape could hold more than one meaning, namely for the funder and the end-user, and we achieved it by fulfilling our part of the bargain to make it work. In doing so, we were supported by our client who invested far more than is the norm.

It was not smooth, but a conversation developed, and the half-completed scheme contains many moves, which were at first rejected but which, by being tried out as temporary moves, stuck: for example, the idea of having many places to sit, which was initially worried over, have been embraced.

We were commissioned in 2010. In 2014, in advance of a building, the first element of the public realm was installed, including a small "mountain"—the stone came from Scotland—every sharp edge rounded to a radial curve for play, a tree selected for its deformities not its straightness, and a stone-paved route lined with planted fences through the site.

In 2015, the art strategy required by the planning permissions was produced. It was a piece of action research, not a written document, but a three-month exploration, named the "Festival of Toil." Led by Katherine Clarke, muf's artist partner working on the construction site itself, the written brief was created through collaborating with a local organization and the young men they work with. The relationship has continued.

The action research explored John Ruskin's proposition that the highest reward for your toil is not what you get for it, but what you become by it. Over three months, the team made their own work clothes, a clay oven from scratch using earth dug from the development site, "sporks" — spoon-fork hybrids, cast from site waste aluminum, and a suite of furniture from the site hoardings. They then used what they had made to host a dinner debate for 30 local decision makers.

The resultant commission, "Every Increased Possession Loads Us with New Weariness" by Revital Cohen and Tuur Van Balen, is a public sculpture for Ruskin Square that reverses the supply chains of the development, unmaking the building and remaking it into an artificial mineral of steel, concrete, glass, aluminum, copper, cast iron, and Caithness stone.

For example, a steel girder was taken from the building and sent back to the factory (Hare in Bury, near Manchester), where workers were asked to unmake the product they would normally make.

The second public space has been under construction since 2016. It includes an oval stage (a direct reference to Ruskin's drawing studio at Great Ormond Street, where his drawing lessons took place), child-sized seats amongst the adult benches, a lion to clamber on, and rich vegetation. A single large chestnut tree was retained on the site with great effort and bloody-mindedness on the part of all involved. The edges of the completed spaces are planted hoardings: part a development site, part a place to spend time. These spaces are both highly controlled and strangely welcoming, perhaps because the buildings are still to come — so many places to sit, a drinking fountain, and nothing to buy. A pause before the rest of the buildings is completed.[7]

Wedge Two
Dalston: Is Anger a Form of Commitment?

The architect is paid to attend a community event where furious residents are trying to be heard. How does the architect make himself or herself useful in a situation like this? In our practice, we have described ourselves as "double agents" as a way of characterizing our response to a brief for public space in a commercial development. We treat the users as our clients rather than the source of our fee. We call this our *duty of care*. Good intentions are not enough. This is a design approach that cannot be *done* to a population or even *for* one.

For a successful afterlife to persist after you have left the scene, your contribution — however well-meaning — requires a significant understanding of the existing situation and, through that, an understanding of who will use it, look after it, and how all this will be funded.

In the project *Making Space in Dalston*, the situation was a neighborhood where the community was doing battle with the local authorities and city-wide plans. We found ourselves there through the usual route of the "loaded" commission. A library with housing above was to replace a building, which had housed the Four Aces Club — a building rich in histories.[8] This was our entry pass, the possibility that gave us a reason to be in the room on the day when the appropriate form of public art commission was being discussed.

The wedge in the door for Dalston was the attempt to slow things down before masterplans, drawn at a distance in expressive and imprecise thick strokes, were put into effect. We did this simply by describing to those in authority what was of value in the here and now. Helping those in power understand the existing value of a place can be a means of ensuring its protection — a shoring up — of a local authority that is in danger of being a supplicant to developers and is too grateful to whatever crumbs of investment they might bring. (Equally and dangerously, this can be a description of potential value that encourages moves to speed up gentrification and displacement).

Our first move to wedge the door open was to make a map of all the sites of cultural activity collected through one-to-one conversations. "Culture," in this case, was defined as the arts and all examples of cultural exchange. Our question — "What do you do?" — was also the building of the invitation list for the monthly meetings during which we developed the project.

It seems absurd that mapping was the necessary stand-in for the experience of being in a place. The mapping contradicted the master-planners' bold felt pen arrow, which made its direct North-South route, drawing over a building with 60 small businesses. Residents, many of whom had fought to be heard at so many meetings for so many years, were initially furious with us, the translators. But in time, trusting relationships were established, and they sat patiently in the room as we presented what was just sitting there in plain sight to those paid to make plans for a neighborhood they did not live in.

Our second way of wedging the door open was to relocate monthly meetings from the council offices to a different room identified on our map each month. The monthly meetings were held in Dalston itself, and we invited the officers who had contributed from a distance to making plans for this place, as if the place were a blank page waiting to be drawn on. Whereas the mapping was the graphic creation of a digestible tidying-up of a place, these meetings in open spaces, a theater, the Alevi Cultural Centre, Centreprise (an Afro-Caribbean community center, since closed) were deliberately immersive. Food was always served, the officials from the mayor's office and the local authorities were hosted, power relations were flipped, and a new relationship was made.

Our focus widened from the mapping exercise to a brief — the development of a list of projects worked out with many of those we had first met through the mapping exercise — and, lastly, to building some of these projects.

The Eastern Curve garden is one of these, a discussed railway marked as a shopping loop in that, is an enclosed communal garden, a small bar, busy in the summer, funds the year long program. The space, designed and built with Nik Henninger, is now run by two of the most furious residents we met at the first mapping stage.

"Making Space in Dalston" (2008—2010) was a rich and collaborative project not least with our co-authors J&L Gibbons. We operated as critics to a masterplan commissioned from expert masterplanners, and were partially successful in slowing it down. The spaces identified with residents got some funding and continue life as shared local spaces. Visitors to Dalston will see that it was only partial and that, alongside the making visible the often hidden social value of the place, the growth in land values through development and commerce also continued apace.

Concluding Question

Is it enough to wedge the door open? Does it make the complicity, the shape-shifting, the endlessly flexible "services" involved in getting the job and getting into the room, any more palatable if you can bring the wedge to share your relative privilege with others?

In 2017, Conservative mayor Boris Johnson was replaced by Labor mayor Sadiq Khan, and so growth was replaced with "Good Growth." The compromises described

fig. 14 We made a garden and installed cricket nets in 2011. With the belief that this could protect the only building on the site a theatre. The theatre was demolished. In 2012 we got agreement for the organisation that supported young unaccompanied asylum seekers to hold a key to the garden. These remained for two years.

above have now been articulated as an ideal — enshrined in the new planning codes as ambitious intent. We shall see what we shall see.

1 The Ghost of Christmas Future from Charles Dickens's *A Christmas Carol.*
2 What comes to mind is the anthropologist in George Perec's *Life: A User's Manual*, who follows a tribe into ever more hostile settings only to realize on his deathbed that they were, in fact, trying to get away from him.
3 Our office rent is approximately 90,000 EUR a year, our landlords are a hospice rather than an off-shore conglomerate (we occupy the building they built as income for their activities), we get some pleasure out of where the money goes.
4 In 2002, mayor Ken Livingston set the aim to provide 100 public spaces for London as part of a program under the same title.
5 The expression "Deep Hanging Out" relates to an approach to ethnography coined by Clifford Geertz, "Deep Hanging Out," The New York Review of Books (October 22, 1998). → https://www.nybooks.com/articles/1998/10/22/deep-hanging-out
6 The term "agent of expensiveness" is inspired by Margaret Crawford, "Can Architects be Socially Responsible?" in *Out of Site, A Social Criticism of Architecture*, ed. Diane Yvonne Ghirardo (Seattle: Bay Press, 1991), 27—45.
7 For illustrations see → http://www.muf.co.uk/portfolio/ruskin-square
8 Read more here → https://issuu.com/mufarchitectureartllp/docs/making_space_big, https://issuu.com/mufarchitectureartllp/docs/layout_final_vis_rev_05

fig. 15—17 “The Festival of Toil”

fig. 18—20 J&L Gibbbons came onto the team. This allowed us to be ambitious to make a landscape which soaked up the rain, to plant mature trees and to grow moments contrived wilderness for the office worker or passer by to retreat to.

Iva Čukić

Building Alternatives: Self-Organization in Cities

When we turn our gaze to the current urban planning dynamics in cities, we find a debate around the production of space covering the scope defined by the two poles of, on the one hand, large and intricately composed concepts of market-driven spatial design and, on the other, the vitality of bottom-up processes. The first one relates to the currently dominant production of urban space, shifting toward economic growth, where financial capital has a major role in shaping cities around the world. In this context, the cities are losing public spaces and social and cultural services in favor of the construction of shopping malls, luxurious office spaces, and residential buildings. Simultaneously, bottom-up processes are emerging across European cities, operating along principles of self-organization in order to challenge the dominant urban reality, where corporate capital has a significant role in the production of space and services.[1]

The turning of the cities toward neoliberal economy implies a commitment to entrepreneurial ideas and to setting up local features in the service of economic growth and competitiveness. Through the general deployment of the term *real estate*, the space serves mostly to promote a *generic* desirability in economic terms.[2] This development, seen in many European countries, was followed by a shift from welfare systems toward the neoliberal policies and practices of extensive privatization,[3] where space is something no longer to use but to own (with the hope of increased asset-value, rather than use-value, over time).[4]

The costs of the financialization of cities amplified along with the economic crisis, and many urban functions have lost their status as sites of welfare or cultural services. These functions become a part of the calculation of a potential buildable size, instead of a potential contribution to the quality of life.[5] Under these conditions, when urban space becomes a target of speculation, communities and self-organized initiatives start seeking the way to reshape cities in a different way than the one put forward by developers, who are backed by finance, corporate capital, and an increasingly entrepreneurially-minded local state apparatus.[6] Nonetheless, with the economic crisis severely hitting the real estate sector, and as the consequence of the political and economic instability, we can notice a growing civil sector, neighborhood initiatives, and community organizations that increasingly take over the city and offer the possibility of bottom-up, more inclusive, and democratic solutions for the reuse of spaces and the provision of social and cultural services.

Such civic responses in times of economic and political upheavals have a long history. In the late 1920s and early 1930s in the wake of the Great Depression, squatter settlements and self-built structures flourished.[7] In the 1980s and 1990s, many European cities faced politically motivated squatting, oriented toward the creation and occupation of spaces for alternative lifestyles and housing models. For example, in Berlin at that time, counter-culture, social movements, and the underground electronic scene established the body of knowledge and developed the capacities to transform unused and abandoned sites into fertile grounds for "a new wave of uncontrolled urban practices and ideas [...] whose restless speed was barely slowed down by formal control mechanisms."[8]

This approach inspired many practitioners, and, since then, the self-organization and occupation of unused spaces has played an important role in shaping European cities. This has been accompanied by the development of neighborhood initiatives, community-led infrastructures, housing rights networks, and ethical financial organizations, occupying a great diversity of positions within the discourse on how cities should evolve.[9] Nowadays, the *do-it-yourself* civic engagement varies from urban gardens and farms,[10] to social and cultural centers and co-working spaces, to the non-profit models of housing or citizen-run health clinics, food centers, kitchens and aid hubs, which have sprung up to fill the gaps left by austerity.

The Emergence of the Right to the City Narrative

The space to maneuver outside the real estate market or state capture is limited and depends on both the political agenda and existing skills for an alternative, innovative, and often confrontational attitude. Self-organized practices that are politically motivated or strongly connected to specific ideological claims usually share a conflicting attitude toward the public administration and local authorities. This relates to the fact that the actors involved do not have the same level of social and political power and influence, including unequal opportunities for involvement in decision-making processes and public resource management. In this respect, self-organized practices and community initiatives follow what David Harvey describes as "a right to change ourselves by changing the city"[11] through appropriation, transformation, and the use of urban infrastructures.[12]

Harvey continues on Lefebvre's concept through the uncompromising criticism of the conditions under which the modern city has been produced.[13] He defines the right to the city as the right to re-create ourselves through the creation of a qualitatively different kind of urban sociality.[14] It is conceived as a collective right of those who inhabit the city to appropriate it as a platform of solidarity of various social struggles,[15] guided by the principle of equality and participation of all actors.[16] A group of Yugoslavian philosophers and sociologists gathering around *The Praxis Journal*[17] closely interpreted Lefebvre's concept. They claimed that the right to the city is a neo-Marxist axiom that can only be achieved through a radical change in the production and property relations, implying the actual use value of space to again become dominant, from which users are alienated because of the prevailing commercial values and strategies of profit. In this context, self-organization (based on the right to appropriate the city) can be understood as a creation of the social backbone for building alternatives, as a specific request for the social, economic, and political goods, housing, culture, and work, which will empower communities and improve the quality of their lives.

In reaction to the lack of affordable housing, different urban actors emerged in cities across North-West Europe.[18] The gradually de-radicalizing squatting movement played an important role in offering alternative housing solutions. For example, former squatters and housing activists in the city of Freiburg formed in 1989 *Mietshäuser Syndikat*, a not-for-profit investment company aiming to support people in organizing their housing arrangements collectively and sustainably at socially sound rent levels.[19] Today, the house syndicate has a network of 127 housing projects across Germany, in self-managed buildings of their own, making them independent of landlords' plans to raise rents, or to demolish or convert buildings. As a part of the network created and managed by the *Syndikat*, all their projects are self-organized and autonomous, yet committed to the idea of solidarity, which prevents any potential re-privatization and commercial exploitation of the houses. Thus, the model created for this housing co-operative presents a strong political structure that was established to prevent property speculations, to secure affordable rents, and to resist the dominant market-driven urbanization.

The consequences of economic instability and austerity measures are mostly visible in South European countries. Spain, for example, has a strong and politicized structure of self-organized movements that emerged from the 15M movement. In opposition to what happened on the state level during the 2016 elections, a strong network of civic initiatives managed to win the elections on the local level in Madrid, Barcelona, and Valencia. Furthermore, they succeeded in developing strategies and new forms of participation, as well as in empowering self-organized civic initiatives.

In the Greek context, in order to respond to social needs, many initiatives decided to operate in parallel or alternative ways, with the strong recognition of non-monetary values. For example, under the exclusionary measures and due to the public health cuts that were pursued in the Greek system, health care workers initiated alternative "social clinics" that provided free primary health care to all, migrants and Greeks, excluded from the National Health Care System since 2011. The austerity measures have fostered self-organization among volunteer doctors, nurses, and administrative assistants, who squat or use buildings donated by the local municipality in order to build a soli-

fig. 21 Ministarstvo prostora — Ministry of Space: Don't let Belgrade D(r)own

darity structure guaranteeing access to care for those who need it. Today, there are approximately 50 solidarity clinics spread all over Greece. They have appeared as a collective social experience based on voluntary work, on solidarity, and in close connection with everyday life.

Various self-organized initiatives around Europe show differences in organizational and management principles, levels of collaboration with the public and/or private sector, accessibility, financial sustainability, autonomy, and the political dimension. Even though, in some cases, they challenge the rules of the neoliberal agenda, public authorities tend to create mechanisms of dependence on the public sector, which, in the long term, makes self-organized practices less resilient and autonomous. While the above mentioned examples are just a few out of many cases presented in various studies and platforms, they can still serve as a resource and inspiration for more resilient future local initiatives. These cases, nevertheless, give evidence to new urban spaces of conflict where collective power forms in resistance to the neoliberal system.

Taking Back the City: The Case of Belgrade

The rapid and recent growth of self-organized practices and movements is noticeable in Serbia as well, especially in its capital city, Belgrade. The collapse of the socialist system, the accompanying universal mantra about privatization and foreign investments as the only way out, and the politics of creating new identities characterize the dominant development paradigm. During more than half a century, changes in the paradigm of development have turned from a socialist centralized model of management and planning, to the chaotic period of the 1990s, only to end with the surrender to the market-driven development rules.

fig. 22 Ministarstvo prostora — Ministry of Space: Don't let Belgrade D(r)own

Therefore, the urban development in Belgrade has been continuously hindered by the political instability, the turbulent socio-economic situation, and the inconsistent planning systems and procedures. The lack of a wide dialogue concerning the desired urban development, therefore, contributes to corruption in urban planning and resource management, construction projects detached from actual needs and plenty of non-utilized public places, abandoned urban structures and commercialized public spaces, and the lack of programs with public benefit and public infrastructure.

Facing this urban reality, the activist collective *Ministry of Space* (*Ministarstvo prostora*) was established in 2010 with the aim to envision a city where citizens would participate in the decision-making processes, where their satisfaction of needs would be carried out through an open dialogue, and where priority would be given to basic common needs regarding the equal access to spatial resources upholding core democratic principles. This collective has been most active within the fields of new forms of politics and movements, commons, and self-organization, experimenting with various approaches in the struggle for a just and open city. In this sense, *Ministry of Space* follows Harvey's ideas of the "right" through appropriation, transformation, and the use of urban infrastructures, with the aim to empower citizens to propose alternatives and to foster networks, self-management, and self-production.

One of the biggest achievements of this collective has been the development of a movement named *Ne da(vi) mo Beograd* (*Don't Let Belgrade D(r)own*), which brings together organizations and individuals interested in sustainable city development, the fair use of common resources, and the involvement of citizens in the urban development of their environment. The movement against the colossal and controversial project *Belgrade Waterfront* mobilized many Belgrade citizens who denounced the high level of non-transparent and usurping maneuvers of privatization and the unprecedented attack on the city and public infrastructure by speculative and megalomaniac investments. For more than three years, this movement has explored non-transparent and non-inclusive procedures by which the central part of Belgrade's waterfront area was appropriated for private investor interests. In Spring—Summer 2016, more than 20,000 citizens gathered to protest the unlawful and still uninvestigated night-time demolitions in Belgrade's Savamala district that took place on April 24—25, 2016.[20] The mass mobilization around this "project of national importance" spread across Belgrade, encouraging citizens to react when confronted with the unwanted development in their neighborhoods and making the issue of planning and participation processes be one of the central incentives of citizen mobilization.

As Harvey argues in his *Rebel Cities*, the misery inflicted by contemporary capitalism and state power needs to be tackled based on the realities of people's everyday lives. The common drive to reclaim everyday life against the neoliberal system was crucial in forming and shaping the political agenda that challenged the rules of the neoliberal mantra. Furthermore, rather than fighting against the City Hall, *Ne da(vi)mo Beograd* decided to enter the political territory on the local level and shake the institutions captured by the political and corporate powers. Even though the movement did not pass the elections on the city level (March 2018), it gained sizable support of the citizens, followed by support from many municipal movements such as *Barcelona en Comu* (Spain), *Zagreb is ours* (Croatia), *Cambiamo Messina dal Basso* (Italy), etc. Hence, the movement's members believe that claiming commons, fighting the further privatization and commodification of public resources and infrastructure, and shifting the balance of the power are the priorities in building alternatives by experimenting with different governance models and practices that would democratize control over public resources and services.

Conclusion

A narrative on the self-organized and self-managed practices, community-led initiatives, bottom-up or grassroots, and commons, has gradually emerged across Europe both on theoretical and practical levels, thereby motivating and mobilizing power that demands a political change and a deep transformation of the governance regime in a more egalitarian and sustainable direction. The key challenge for self-organized initiatives is to decipher the causes and consequences of the market-driven urbanization and the possibility for alternative, radical, and progressive responses. In Harvey's view, a key task is to chart the path toward an alternative post-capitalist form of urbanization. In this context, self-organized practices are not only a response to the neoliberal urban development but also the way to establish new and productive relations between different social, political, economic, and cultural elements. Moreover, they build alternatives expressing the real needs of citizens instead of those fostered by the political or corporate powers.

There are many exemplary cases (struggles for affordable housing across Europe, self-organized practices and municipal platforms emerging in South-East Europe, struggles rooted in exploitation of nature, and pressure on public resources) that show increasing reactions to the economic crisis, which cannot be separated from the political one. Hence, they can be crucial in shaping a political agenda that challenges the rules of the neoliberal agenda. From this perspective, these practices can be seen as principles on how we want to share, produce, own, or accumulate: by establishing new social relations that build on and help to articulate political discourse in urban space. In this way, self-organized practices and the emergence of commons are calls to construct our future in a collective and democratic manner by proposing alternatives that aim to be both radical and realistic.

1 Several works published in the 1960s and 1970s on the informal and unplanned processes serve as a valuable impulse for the renewal of the urban planning process. In recent years the development of the theoretical discourse about the phenomenon of self-organized initiatives and practices, based on the principles of DIY philosophy dealing with the city, has been noticeable.
2 Reinier De Graaf, "Architecture is Now a Tool of Capital, Complicit in a Purpose Antithetical to its Social Mission," *The Architectural Review* (2015).
→ https://www.architectural-review.com/rethink/viewpoints/architecture-is-now-a-tool-of-capital-complicit-in-a-purpose-antithetical-to-its-social-mission/8681564.article.
3 Christian Grauvogel, "With the Capital against Speculation: New Institutions and Cooperative Finance in Times of Austerity," in *Funding Cooperative City: Community Finance and the Economy of Civic Spaces*, eds. Daniella Patti and Levente Polyak (Vienna: Cooperative City Books, 2017), 45—50.
4 De Graaf, "Architecture."
5 Daniela Patti and Levente Polyak, "From Top-Down Planning through Speculative Developments to Community Economy," in *Funding Cooperative City: Community Finance and the Economy of Civic Spaces*, eds. Daniella Patti and Levente Polyak (Vienna: Cooperative City Books, 2017), 13—21.
6 David Harvey, "The Right to the City," *New Left Review* 53 (2008): 34.
7 Klaus Overmeyer, ed., *Urban Pioneers. Berlin: Stadtenwiclung durch Zwishenmutzung / Temporary Use and Urban Development in Berlin* (Berlin: Senatsverwaltung fur Stadtenwicklung, 2007).
8 Kenny Cupers and Markus Miessen. *Spaces of Uncertainty* (Wuppertal: Müller and Busmann, 2002), 78.
9 Ethical financial organizations or ethical banks operate ethically both in terms of their internal and external mode of operation by functioning in the interest of local communities and providing financial services to projects such as affordable housing, education, and culture. See: Daniella Patti and Levente Polyak, eds., Funding Cooperative City: Community Finance and the Economy of Civic Spaces (Vienna: Cooperative City Books, 2017), 238.
10 The use of unused urban land for gardens and smaller farms has significantly increased over the past few years. See Mike Lyndon, Tactical Urbanism, Volume 1 (March 13, 2012).
→ http://issuu.com/streetplanscollaborative/docs/tactical_urbanism_vol.1, Mike Lyndon, Tactical Urbanism, Volume 2 (March 2, 2012):
→ http://issuu.com/streetplanscollaborative/docs/tactical_urbanism_vol_2_final, Peter Bishop and Lesley Williams, The Temporary City (Oxon: Routledge, 2012), Philipp Oswalt, Klaus Overmeyer, and Philipp Misselwitz, Urban Catalyst – Planning of the Unprojectable (Berlin: dom publishers, 2013),
→ http://urbancatalyst.net/, Such spaces, often completely vacant and abandoned, have been occupied regardless of whether they are public or private property. For an overview and the history of the phenomenon, see Elke Krasny, ed. The Right to Green: Hands-on Urbanism 1850—2012 (Hong Kong: MCCM Creations, 2014).
11 Harvey, "The Right."
12 Constantin Petcou and Doina Petrescu, "R-Urban or How to Co-Produce a Resilient City (1st excerpt)," in *Build the City. Perspectives on Commons and Culture*, eds. Charles Beckett, Lore Gablier, Vivian Paulissen, Igor Stokfiszewski, and Joanna Tokarz-Haertig (Amsterdam, Warsaw:

The European Cultural Foundation and Krytyka Polityczna, 2015), 153—157.

13 Henri Lefebvre, "Pravo na grad / The Right to the City," in *Operacija grad: Priručnik za život u neoliberalnoj stvarnosti*, eds. Leonardo Kovačević, Tomislav Medak, Petar Milat, Tonči Valentić, and Vesna Vuković (Zagreb: Savez za centar za nezavisnu kulturu i mlade, Multimedijalni institut, Platforma 9, 81-Institut za istraživanja u arhitekturi, BLOK-Lokalna baza za osvježavanje kulture, SU Klubtura, 2008), 16—30.

14 Harvey, "The Right."

15 The struggle is not limited to a single social category. It can incorporate a diverse range of identities and political interests (to challenge a capitalist city, a racist city, a homophobic city, a patriarchal city, etc.).

16 Lefebvre, "Pravo na grad."

17 The Praxis Journal was a philosophical journal of the Croatian Philosophical Society, in which many eminent, mostly Marxist-oriented, theorists and critics published their works. Among them are the names of famous philosophers and intellectuals from and outside Yuoslavia (Antonio Gramsci, Herbert Marcuse, Erich Fromm, Henri Lefebvre, Jürgen Habermas). The first issue of the magazine was published in 1964. It was stopped in 1974 due to the lack of financial resources and the resistance of the official policy to the critical position of the magazine.

18 In most European countries, long-term housing affordability emerges both at the grassroots and legal levels. The model was created in 1969 in the USA and flourished in the 1990s thanks to the favorable policies and funding environment. The Community Land Trust (CLT) model — a self-organized community-led development where local organizations come together to address housing issues — started receiving attention in several European cities. CLTs, as membership-based, non-profit organizations, provide and encourage the development of affordable housing, community gardens, and civic spaces, while, at the same time, protecting users, residents, and wider community from property speculation.

19 Ko Gradi Grad. *Housing from Below: A Smarter Building Model for Affordable Housing in Serbia* (Belgrade: Ko Gradi Grad, 2017).
→ https://rs.boell.org/sites/default/files/housing_from_below-ko_gradi_grad.pdf.

20 During the night of April 24–25, men wearing balaclavas used excavators to tear down buildings in Hercegovacka Street in Savamala and abused the citizens they encountered nearby. The police failed to respond to calls from neighborhood residents urging them to intervene. The city government was accused of deliberately suspending the rule of law in one part of the city for several hours to enable the de- molitions. More to follow on media reports:
→ https://www.theguardian. com/world/2016/may/26/serbs- rally-against-shady-demolitions-after- masked-crew-tied-up-witnesses,
→ https://www.dw.com/en/covert-demolitions-inspire-opposition-revolt-in-belgrade/a-19266900.

HEINDL/KLEIN/LINORTNER

• Figure 1, page 8
Image: Gabu Heindl, 2015

EYAL WEIZMAN

• Figure 2, page 56
Image: Forensic Architecture, 2016
• Figure 3, page 62
Image: Forensic Architecture, 2017
• Figure 4, page 62
Image: Forensic Architecture and Anderson Acoustics, 2017

KOLOWRATNIK/POINTL

• Figure 5, page 70
Image: Birgit Miksch, 2015
• Figure 6, page 73
Image: Johannes Puchleitner, 2016
• Figure 7, page 74
Image: Anton Wagner and Mario Weisböck, 2015
• Figure 8, page 76
Image: Enrico Weiser, 2016
• Figure 9, page 80
Image: Lea Soltau, 2015

PELIN TAN

• Figure 10, page 94
Image: Pelin Tan, 2015

MATTEO TRENTINI

• Figure 11, page 102
Image: Christina Linortner, 2018

CHRISTIAN KÜHN

• Figure 12, page 116
Source: https://de.wikipedia.org/wiki/Datei:Bundesarchiv_Bild_183-H29710,_Berlin-Friedrichsfelde,_Revolutionsdenkmal.jpg, 1926

LIZA FIOR

• Figure 13, page 147
Image: muf, 2012
• Figure 14, page 159
Image: muf, 2012
• Figure 15, page 161
Image: Martina Ferrera, 2016

- Figure 16, page 162
  Image: Martina Ferrera, 2016
- Figure 17, page 163
  Image: Martina Ferrera, 2016
- Figure 18, page 164
  Image: Lewis Ronald, 2018
- Figure 19, page 165
  Image: Jim Stephenson, 2014
- Figure 20, page 166
  Image: Lewis Ronald, 2018

IVA ČUKIĆ

- Figure 21, page 172
  Source: Inicijativa Ne da(vi)mo Beograd, https://nedavimobeograd.wordpress.com, 2016
- Figure 22, page 174
  Source: Inicijativa Ne da(vi)mo Beograd, https://nedavimobeograd.wordpress.com, 2016

IVA ČUKIĆ

is a co-founder and coordinator of the NGO Ministarstvo prostora collective (Ministry of Space), a do-tank that connects social activists, artists, architects, scholars, and citizens by organizing platforms aiming to research, make models, and conduct campaigns that focus on city development issues. Their activities span from creating independent social and cultural centers to researching and developing policy recommendations on urban planning and public property management. She is a PhD candidate at the Faculty of Architecture, University of Belgrade and, since 2014, a Belgrade team leader/researcher for the New Metropolitan Mainstream INURA project, Zurich.

LIZA FIOR

is a founding partner of muf architecture/art, a London-based practice that negotiates between the built and social fabric. muf was awarded the 2008 European Prize for Public Space for the new town square for Barking (UK) and authored the British Pavilion at Venice Biennale 2010. One of London mayor's Design Advocates, Fior currently teaches the M ARCH "Not a Clean Slate" seminar at Central Saint Martins and is an external examiner for the architecture course at Cambridge University. She co-authored *More than One (Fragile) Thing at a Time*, a project initiated with an award from the Graham Foundation, and *This Is What We Do: A muf Manual* (Batsford Ltd., 2001). www.morethanonefragile.co.uk

FORENSIC ARCHITECTURE (FA),

a research agency based at Goldsmiths, University of London, undertakes advanced spatial and media research on behalf of international prosecutors, human rights organizations, as well as political and environmental justice groups. FA analyzes violations of human rights and international humanitarian law (IHL) in urban, media-rich environments by modeling such dynamic events as they unfold in space and time, which results in the creation of navigable 3D models of conflict sites and of animations and interactive cartographies on the urban or architectural scale. FA's partners have included human rights organizations, such as Amnesty International, Human Rights Watch, Centro para la Acción Legal en Derechos Humanos, B'tselem, Al Mezan, and Migeurop, as well as international prosecutors, international offices, such as the UN Special Rapporteur for Counter-Terrorism and Human Rights, and reporters from The Intercept and the Bureau of Investigative Journalism. FA shares their work with the public through publications, exhibitions, and presentations at leading research and cultural institutes. It is essential for Forensic Architecture's practice to always have as the main beneficiaries of their work the victims of human rights violations and communities either in conflict zones or otherwise subject to state failure or violence.

GABU HEINDL

is an architect, urbanist, and theorist based in Vienna. She obtained her post-professional master degree at Princeton University and a PhD from the Academy of Fine Arts in Vienna. Her architectural studio, GABU Heindl Architecture, specializes in public space, public/social buildings, collective housing, and urban planning. In 2013—2017, she was the chairwoman of The Austrian Society for Architecture (ÖGFA). Heindl is the author of numerous publications and the curator of exhibitions and symposia. She lectures and publishes internationally on politics of housing/urban planning with regard to popular agency. She was the editor of *Arbeit Zeit Raum. Bilder und Bauten der Arbeit im Postfordismus* (Turia+Kant, 2008). Her forthcoming book *Stadtkonflikte* (*City conflicts*) connects architecture and urban planning to the political theory of radical democracy. Since 2018 Visiting Professor an der Sheffield University, since 2019 Diploma Unit Master, AA London.

ANA JEINIĆ

was born 1981 in Banjaluka, SFR Yugoslavia. She studied architecture and philosophy in Graz, Venice, and Delft. Upon graduating at Graz University of Technology, she has mainly worked as an architectural theorist and educator. She co-edited the volume *Is There (Anti)Neoliberal Architecture?* (2013), led the curatorial project "Architecture After the Future" (2016/17), and published numerous articles, essays, and speculations about architecture, landscape, islands, and utopias. Currently, she is finalizing her doctoral thesis at the Institute of Architectural Theory, Art History, and Cultural Studies in Graz.

MICHAEL KLEIN

works at the intersections of architecture, urbanism, art, and cultural theory, currently at the Department of Housing and the Department of Urban Design at TU Wien, as well as for *dérive* (journal for urban research) and the ÖGFA (the Austrian Society for Architecture). Major topics include housing and everyday life, as well as history and political theory. His works include *The Design of Scarcity*, (co-authored with Jon Goodbun, Andreas Rumpfhuber and Jeremy Till, Strelka Press, 2014), *Modelling Vienna — Real Fictions in Social Housing*, (co-authored with Andreas Rumpfhuber, Turia+Kant 2015) as well as a film *60 Elephants. Episodes of a Theory* (co-directed with Sasha Pirker, 2018).

NINA VALERIE KOLOWRATNIK

is an architect and researcher currently based in Vienna. Her practice is situated in the context of forced migration and claims to land and property, and develops spatial notational systems that operate within debates on human rights. Since 2014, she has been teaching graduate courses on borderlands, migration, and counter narratives at Columbia University GSAPP and TU Vienna. Her forthcoming book *The Language of Secret Proof* (published by Sternberg Press) is a research project on evidence-production within Native American land claims. Recently, her work has been shown at Stacion CCA Prishtina, the Venice Architecture Biennale, and the Oslo Architecture Triennale. She is the recipient of the Outstanding Artist Award in Experimental Tendencies in Architecture 2016. Kolowratnik holds an MArch from TU Graz and an MS in Critical, Curatorial, and Conceptual Practices in Architecture from Columbia University.

CHRISTIAN KÜHN

was born in 1962 in Vienna. Kühn studied at TU Wien (Dipl. Ing.) and ETH Zurich (Dr. sc. techn.). Teaching at TU Wien since 1989, he became University Professor in 2001. He is also the chairman of the Austrian Architectural Foundation (since 2000) and was a member of the OECD Working Group for Educational Buildings in 2005—2011. His research areas include history and theory of architecture, and social infrastructure with the focus on educational facilities. Kühn is an architectural critic for various newspapers and journals (such as *Architektur- und Bauforum*, *ARCH+*, *Merkur*, *Die Presse*). He has been chairman of the board for “Baukultur” in the Austrian Federal Chancellery since 2015. He co-authored *Austrian Report on Building Culture* (2006, 2011, 2017). He was the Austrian Pavillion commissioner and curator for Venice Architecture Biennale 2014.

CHRISTINA LINORTNER

is an architect and has been a Teaching Fellow and Research Associate at TU Graz since 2013. She studied Architecture at TU Vienna and Research Architecture at Goldsmiths College, London. She has done transdisciplinary work in the areas of migration, housing culture, and transcultural studies. She has been a board member at the Austrian Society for Architecture (ÖGFA) since 2014. She has worked in the field of artistic research, as well as in architectural practices in London, Rotterdam, and Vienna, amongst others. Since 2005, she has been involved in exhibition, publication, and project activities, mainly focusing on the interface between architecture, research, and art.

JOHANNES POINTL
is a practicing architect and urban designer, as well as Assistant Professor at TU Wien. He obtained his post-professional master degree in Urban Design at GSAPP, Columbia University in New York, and a professional degree in architecture from Graz University of Technology, Austria. Pointl has worked as a project manager for architecture and urban design offices in Berlin, New York and Vienna and taught design studios at GSAPP and Vienna University of Technology. He has realized architectural projects in Austria, Italy, and Greece with his independent practice and has contributed to and edited publications on urban design in Austrian, Belgium, Germany, Haiti, and Ghana. Pointl's current work deals with the intersection of social housing and urban design policies.

JANE RENDELL's
research, writing, and pedagogic practice crosses architecture, art, feminism, history, and psychoanalysis. She has introduced concepts of "critical spatial practice" and "site-writing" through her authored books: *The Architecture of Psychoanalysis* (2017), *Silver* (2016), *Site-Writing* (2010), *Art and Architecture* (2006), and *The Pursuit of Pleasure* (2002). Her co-edited collections include *Reactivating the Social Condenser* (2017), *Critical Architecture* (2007), *Spatial Imagination* (2005), *The Unknown City* (2001), *Intersections* (2000), *Gender, Space, Architecture* (1999) and *Strangely Familiar* (1995). Jane is Professor of Architecture and Art at the Bartlett School of Architecture, University College London, where she co-initiated the new Situated Practice MA programme and supervises PhDs in architecture, art, urbanism, and experimental writing. Working with Dr. David Roberts, Bartlett Ethics Fellow, she leads the Bartlett's Ethics Commission, and Ethics Work Package for KNOW (Knowledge in Action for Urban Equality), together with Dr. Yael Padan, Research Associate. In 2018, she was awarded the History/Theory prize at the RIBA Research Awards for her work on housing and psychoanalysis and the Provost's Education Award for her work on ethics.
www.janerendell.co.uk

RUTH SONDEREGGER
teaches Philosophy and Aesthetic Theory at the Academy of Fine Arts Vienna. Her main fields of research are (the colonial history of) aesthetics, critical theories, and resistance studies. Among her recent publications are: *Conceptions of Critique in Modern and Contemporary Philosophy* (co-edited with Karin de Boer, 2012), *Art and the Critique of Ideology After 1989* (co-edited with Eva Birkenstock, Max Hinderer, and Jens Kastner, 2013), *Pierre Bourdieu und Jacques Rancière. Ästhetisches Regime oder ästhetische Disposition?*

(co-edited with Jens Kastner, 2014), *Spaces for Criticism. Contemporary Art Discourses* (co-edited with Pascals Gielen, Thijs Lijster, and Suzana Milevska, 2015), *Foucaults Gegenwart. Sexualität — Sorge — Revolution* (co-authors: Gundula Ludwig and Isabell Lorey, 2016), *Vom Leben der Kritik* (Wien: Zaglossus, 2019).

PELIN TAN

is a sociologist and art historian. She was a visiting professor at the architecture faculty of University of Cyprus in Nicosia, 2018 and Hong Kong Polytechnic School of Design, 2016. She was also Associate Professor and Vice-Dean of Architecture Faculty, Mardin Artuklu University, Turkey, 2013—2017. She is a lead author of chapter "Towards an Urban Society" (*International Panel on Social Progress*, edited by Saskia Sassen and Edgar Pieterse, Cambridge Press, 2018). Tan has also contributed to *2000+: Urgencies of Architectural Theories* (GSAPP, 2015), *Climates: Architecture and The Planetary Imaginary* (Lars Muller & Columbia Univ., 2017), *Position on Emancipation — Architecture between Aesthetics and Politics* (Lars Muller, 2018), *Radical Geography Notebook* (Athens, 2017), and *Swamps and the New Imagination* (MIT Press, 2019). She is a member of the curatorial board of IBA Stuttgart 2027, as well as the curator of Matera ECC 2019. Tan is a member of the pedagogical consortium of Campus in Camp, Palestine.

MATTEO TRENTINI,

architect, obtained his PhD in History and Theory of Architecture in 2018 at Accademia di Architettura in Mendrisio (CH), where he was a teaching assistant at the chair of Architectural Theory and History of Modern Architecture in 2013—2018. Since 2014, he has taught a seminar on postwar architecture in Germany and Italy. Since 2018, he has been a research associate at Institut für Grundlagen moderner Architektur und Entwerfen (IGMA), University of Stuttgart. He has published in journals such as *Costruire*, *Il Giornale dell'Architettura*, and *Il Manifesto*.

Building Critique — Architecture and its Discontents

Editors: Gabu Heindl, Michael Klein, Christina Linortner
Co-editor: ÖGFA — Österreichische Gesellschaft für Architektur

Graphic Design: CH Studio, Christian Hoffelner
Type Design: Fabian Harb, Dinamo
Copyediting and Proofreading: Rafal Morusiewicz
Printing and Binding: druckhaus köthen GmbH & Co. KG

Published by: Spector Books
Harkortstraße 10, 04107 Leipzig
www.spectorbooks.com

Distribution:
• Germany, Austria: GVA, Gemeinsame Verlagsauslieferung Göttingen GmbH & Co. KG, www.gva-verlage.de
• Switzerland: AVA Verlagsauslieferung AG, www.ava.ch
France, Belgium: Interart Paris, www.interart.fr
• UK: Central Books Ltd, www.centralbooks.com
• USA, Canada, Central and South America, Africa, Asia: ARTBOOK | D.A.P., www.artbook.com
• South Korea: The Book Society, www.thebooksociety.org
• Australia, New Zealand: Perimeter Distribution, www.perimeterdistribution.com

Federal Chancellery
Republic of Austria

Österreichische Gesellschaft
für Architektur

First edition
Printed in Germany

ISBN 978-3-95905-237-5